Todi Walking Tours

Todi Walking Tours

Walking-Tour Guide for English-Speaking Visitors

Bernard Mansheim &
Claudio Peri

gatekeeper press
Columbus, Ohio

Todi Walking Tours:
Walking-Tour Guide for English-Speaking Visitors

Published by Gatekeeper Press
2167 Stringtown Rd, Suite 109
Columbus, OH 43123-2989
www.GatekeeperPress.com

Copyright © 2018 by Bernard Mansheim
and Claudio Peri

All rights reserved. Neither this book, nor any parts within it may be sold or reproduced in any form or by any electronic or mechanical means, including information storage and retrieval systems without permission in writing from the author. The only exception is by a reviewer, who may quote short excerpts in a review.

ISBN: 9781642371253
eISBN: 9781642371260

Printed in the United States of America

*We dedicate this book to our dear wives,
Denise and Teresa, who have supported and
encouraged us throughout its development*

Contents

Preface xi
Introduction 1

Part I: Geographic and Historic Features of Todi

Chapter 1: Geography 9
Chapter 2: Todi History 13
    The Umbrian-Etruscan Period 13
    (1,000 BC–300 BC) 13
    The Roman Period (300 BC–AD 400) 16
    Early Middle Ages (6th–11th centuries AD) 18
    High and Late Middle Ages
    (11th–14th centuries AD) 19
    The Renaissance (15th–17th centuries AD) 22
    Modern Age 24

Part II: Points of Interest (POI)

POI-1. Jacopone da Todi 25
POI-2. Teatro Comunale 27
POI-3. Piazza del Popolo 28
POI-4. The Cathedral 31

POI-5. Palazzo Cesi..35
POI-6. Angelo Cesi 36
POI-7. Bishop's Palace..39
POI-8. Renaissance Palaces and Lordships...................40
POI-9. Palazzo del Capitano del Popolo 41
POI-10. Palazzo del Popolo.....................................43
POI-11. Mars Statue...44
POI-12. Palazzo dei Priori.......................................46
POI-13. Eagle's Nest Legend 47
POI-14. Piazza Garibaldi...47
POI-15. San Fortunato Church 50
POI-16. Jacopone da Todi Lyceum 54
POI-17. La Rocca and San Callisto Cistern 56
POI-18. The Medieval Walls and Gates......................57
POI-19. Porta Perugina and Borgo Nuovo 60
POI-20. The Agricultural High School.......................61
POI-21. Medieval Houses and Neighborhood 62
POI-22. Monastery of the Poor Clares and the Purgatorio Painting..64
POI-23. Waterworks and Fonte Scannabecco 66
POI-24. Palazzo Pongelli 68
POI-25. Sant' Ilario..69
POI-26. Nicchioni and Roman Sustaining Structures.71

POI-27. The Roman Amphitheater and the churches of San Filippo and San Nicolò 72

POI-28. Mezzomuro 74

POI-29. Tempio della Consolazione 75

POI-30. The Church of Santa Maria in Camuccia 78

Part III: Walking Tours

Introduction

Tour Route 1. Piazza del Popolo 89

Tour Route 2. From Porta Perugina to
Piazza del Popolo 97

Tour Route 3. From Porta Romana to
Piazza del Popolo 103

Tour Route 4. From Tempio della Consolazione and
Porta Fratta to Piazza del Popolo 109

Part IV: Interesting Historic Sites Near Todi

Introduction 113

Montesanto 114

Carsulae 115

Petrified Forest 116

Notable Villages and Castles Near Todi: 118

References

Acknowledgments 123

Preface

Since Claudio and I published our walking tour book in 2018, Denise and I have returned to Todi on several occasions. Unfortunately, due to COVID-19 restrictions we were unable to return from 2019 until several months ago.

Todi remains a peaceful, noble hill town, whose inhabitants continue to welcome visitors. For example, one evening we dined at our favorite pizza restaurant and the waiter recognized and greeted us with a warm *benvenuto* after an absence of almost four years! Late at night after a stroll through the piazza del popolo, crowds of people of all ages still gather, talking and laughing, enjoying a gelato on the piazza adjacent to the Fonte Cesia

We took the opportunity to traverse the four tours described in the book, which allowed us to make a few minor changes. I am pleased to report that Todi has largely remained the same—no surprise for a town that was colonized over 2,500 years ago.

Two important updates of our tour guide bear mentioning. First, thanks to extensive research by Claudio regarding the famous Todi cleric, fra Jacopone (see **POI-1**), a myth has been debunked. The story about his conversion from a life as a prominent attorney to a dedicated existence as a humble, religious man that we chronicled in the first edition, turns out to be apocryphal. What remains true is the fact that Jacopone did dedicate his life to preaching the teachings of Christ in the Franciscan tradition. His reputation as a holy man and his famous *laudi* (religious poems) have remained with us since his death in AD 1306.

The second important update to our book is recognition of the installation of the Beverly Pepper Sculpture Garden. In 2019 the citizens of Todi honored Beverly Pepper, who lived for fifty years near Todi, now deceased, one of the most prominent sculptors in American history, by dedicating a pathway from the Parca la Rocca down to the Tempio della Consolazione to display twenty of her remarkable works (see **POI-17**).

A few other minor changes have been made to update our tour guide. Overall, Todi remains a true marvel and a proud representative of rich Italian history. Once again, I will close my comments by saying on behalf of Claudio and myself, enjoy your visit.

Arrivederci!
—Bernard Mansheim
March 2024

Introduction

TODI IS A town in Umbria, one of the twenty regions of Italy, and the only land-locked region on the Italian peninsula. Umbria is located in the very center of Italy and the hill town Todi is in the center of Umbria. Three other regions border Umbria: Tuscany to the north and west, Marche to the east, and Lazio to the south. This rural, peaceful, lush region has been called *il cuore verde d'Italia*—the green heart of Italy. (Further discussion of the geographic features of this special place are detailed in Part I, Chapter 1).

The earliest known inhabitants of Umbria were the Umbri people, after whom the region was named. Little is known about the Umbri except for evidence that they colonized central and northern Italy as far back as the Bronze Age, at least 1,000 BC. History tells us that the Etruscans invaded the area between 700-500 BC, but the two peoples seem to have co-existed until the Roman invasion about 300 BC.

Before the Romans, the Etruscans mainly settled the land west of the Tiber River, while the Umbrians remained on the eastern side. Todi played a special role during this time, as it interfaced between the two cultures.

With the collapse of the Roman Empire in the 5th century AD, Umbria came under the control of a succession of invading conquerors. When Charlemagne was crowned emperor of the Holy Roman Empire in AD 800, all of Italy and much of western Europe became unified. At that time, Umbria was declared part of the Papal States. Todi was one of many cities throughout Italy that became somewhat autonomous and were known as *comuni* (municipalities).

For the next ten centuries, the papacy ruled, except for a few decades of Napoleonic rule in the early 1800s. In 1861, Italy became unified as a kingdom, and Umbria was named one of the twenty administrative divisions, known as *regioni*.

As a consequence of the long papal domination, the Catholic religion had a major influence on the culture of Todi. The religious and cultural movements led by Saint Francis and Saint Clare of Assisi, only thirty miles north, reached Todi. Fra Jacopone, arguably the most famous religious poet in Italian history, was a Todi native and followed the mystic tradition of the 13th century.

It is widely known that all of Italy is filled with historic remnants and artifacts dating back nearly 3,000 years. Scattered ruins throughout the country have been found and attributed to the Umbrians, Etruscans, Romans, and other populations and civilizations throughout history. What, then, makes Todi special?

The Umbrian hill town known as Todi serves as the very embodiment of Italian history and culture in a number of ways. Its geographic location, precisely in the center of Italy, had major significance over the millennia, and will be detailed in a later chapter. Of particular note, Todi evolved at the crossroads of six civilizations: Umbrian, Etruscan, Roman, Christian, Medieval, and Renaissance!

Three concentric sets of walls that define the three

major historic eras—Etruscan, Roman, and Medieval—surround Todi. However, the Etruscan walls were subsumed by the Romans, who used Etruscan stonework to establish their formidable walls. Thus, to be accurate, two easily identifiable sets of walls can be seen today.

Despite expansion of Todi's population over the past century, virtually all the newer buildings have been constructed below the lower ring of walls that circumscribe the old city. Thus, Todi has retained a historic structural integrity that is arguably the most untarnished among all the ancient towns of its size in Italy. Though today the existing buildings in the old city almost uniformly reflect construction during the medieval and Renaissance ages, they were built on top of the Roman city, which was in turn built over the original Umbrian/Etruscan city.

As implied above, logically the construction of massive stone monuments during a given civilization was generally preceded by destruction of monuments of the previous civilization, so that the stones and building artifacts that had been laboriously hauled up the long hill could be re-purposed. Following the end of the Roman era, those same elements were used to build the new wall, the *palazzi* (palaces), other housing, churches, and public buildings.

For example, throughout Todi, the magnificent buildings of the Middle Ages and Renaissance are still visible. Beneath the central Piazza del Popolo lie the original Roman cisterns, and the main cathedral stands on top of a former Roman temple. On the streets descending from the main piazza, remnants of Roman and Etruscan tombs and remains are still found occasionally.

Finally, pyramidal-shaped Todi offers a 360-degree panoramic view of the colorful hills, valleys, and distant mountains of Umbria, where visibility can stretch for fifty kilometers (thirty miles) or more in any direction.

We have divided this walking tour guide into several parts with the intent to provide a historical context for an educational hike through this unique town.

Part I offers a more detailed understanding of Todi's place in six major historical periods, beginning with Umbrian/Etruscan times, through three millennia into modern times. Part I provides a backdrop that will inform the walking tourist about the many historic points of interest through the town. It is divided into two chapters. Chapter 1 focuses on the geographic features that have made Todi a unique community over the centuries. Many topics are detailed in this chapter: the location of Todi in central Italy—a part of the country that was a massive lake dating back five million years; why it was founded on a hill along the Tiber River; how it survived clashes between warring civilizations; and what contribution it made to the various cultures that allowed it to remain alive and largely intact for so long. Chapter 2 places Todi into historical perspective, dividing the fascinating story into the major eras that impacted the town over countless centuries. These range from the Umbrian-Etruscan period, through the Roman era, followed by the medieval and Renaissance time periods, and into the modern era.

Part II includes thirty detailed Points of Interest (POI).

Visitors can choose to see specific POIs on their own or to read about the POIs as they follow one or more of the four tour routes. The POIs are described in sufficient detail to stimulate thought, but are not discussed in encyclopedic detail. A number of photographs with captions have been embedded throughout Part II.

Part III details four specific tour routes. Before each route is a map that identifies pertinent POIs along an easily identifiable route. These tours have been developed to capture the essence of Todi throughout the ages.

Part IV provides information on selected nearby historic places of interest, all within thirty miles of Todi. It is a fascinating compilation that includes sites dating from pre-historic times through the Roman, medieval and Renaissance eras.

At the end we have listed two useful references for the visitor who seeks further detailed information on the intriguing story of Todi.

We hope you enjoy your journey as much as we have in preparation of this guide to help you on your way!

—Bernard Mansheim
Claudio Peri

PART I

Geographic and Historic Features of Todi

CHAPTER 1
Geography

THE REGION OF Umbria is in the center of Italy. Todi is in the center of Umbria. In less than two hours, the Adriatic Sea can be reached to the east; the Tyrrhenian Sea is the same distance to the west. In about the same amount of time, Rome can be reached to the southwest and Florence to the north.

Todi is perched on the top of a gentle hill, surrounded by olive groves, vineyards, and sunflower fields. The lowest set of walls that surrounds the ancient town sits part way up the hill. From there the roads lead another 200 meters (650 feet) uphill to the central plaza known as Piazza del Popolo.

From the top set of walls, the Tiber River is visible as it flows lazily from the northwest side of Todi, south toward Rome. To the east, one can see Mount Martani in the distance, a peak of about 3,500 feet, part of the Appenine mountain range that runs north and south through Italy, creating separate meteorological conditions on the Adriatic and Tyrrhenian sides. Along the western side in the distance is the Amerini mountain range. The mountains form a natural protective shield from extreme weather, making Todi and its surrounding countryside a temperate, comfortable place to live.

Over 3,000 years ago, the earliest known inhabitants of Todi, the Umbri, established the town in a perfect defensive location on the top of the hill overlooking

MARTANI
MOUNTAIN

Figure 1. Sketch of original water source that allowed Todi's development on a hilltop.

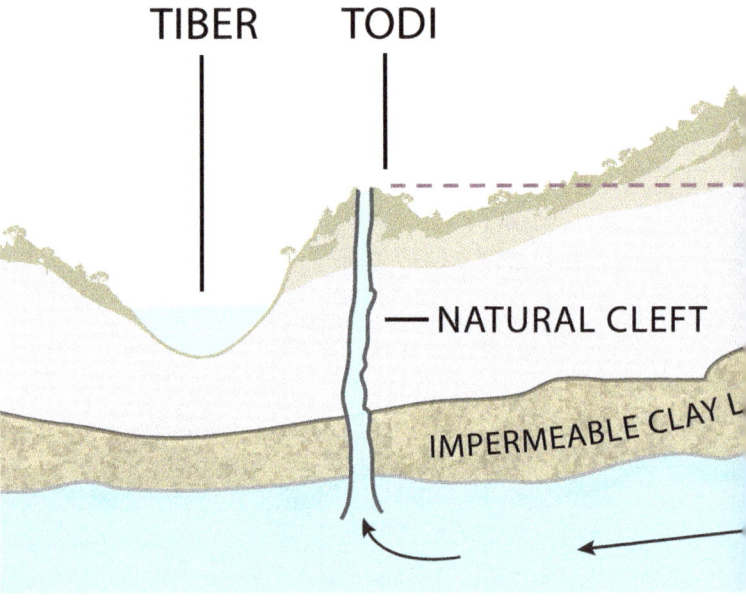

the Tiber River. In addition, its distance above the riverbed far below provided protection from flooding as well as mosquito and other insect infestation. Though many ancient, tiny villages were eventually built in mountainous locations throughout Umbria and

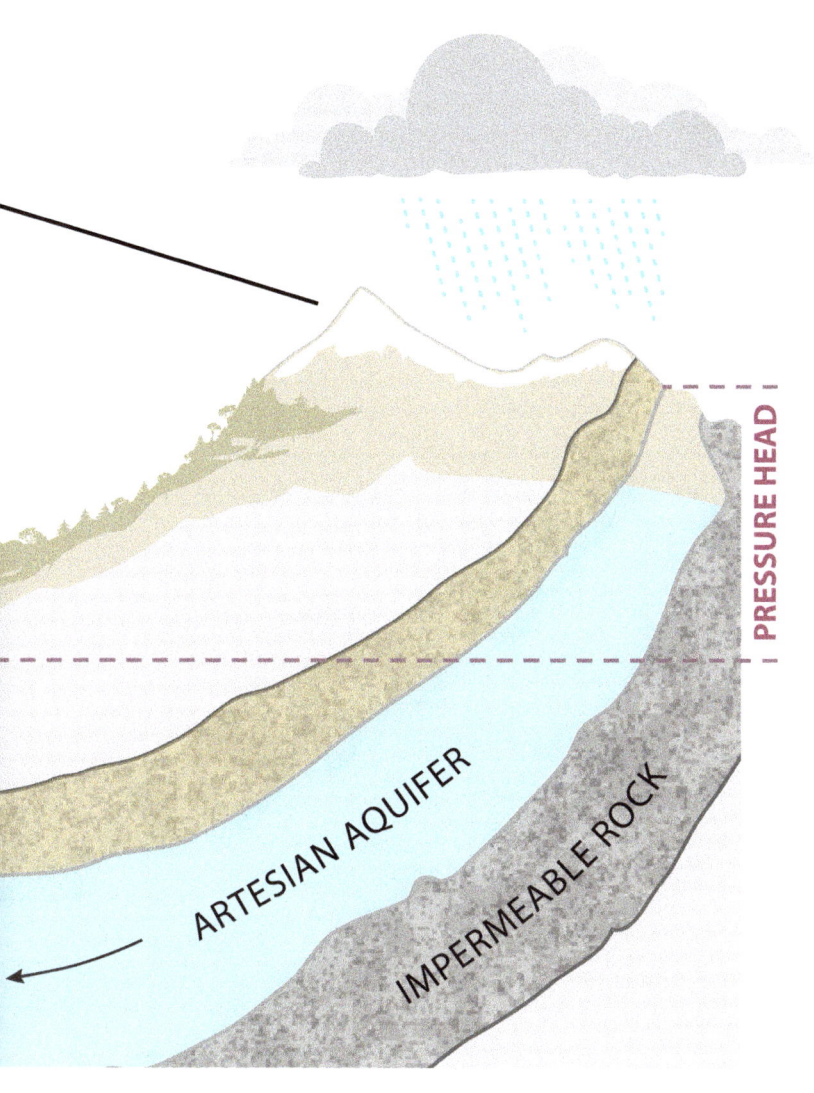

surrounding regions, Todi had a unique feature that assured its success; namely, a series of artesian wells were discovered wherein water literally bubbled up through the ground at the top of the hill.

A further look at Todi shows that the town was

actually built between two hills, separated by a shallow valley that the Roman engineers ingeniously connected by creating the central city forum, underneath which they created a massive water reservoir. Over many centuries as one civilization evolved into another, buildings, temples, churches, public spaces and homes were built on top of the rubble of prior cultures. Today, most of the architecture reflects structures built during the Middle Ages and Renaissance, though remnants of prior civilizations still exist. Details are discussed in the various POIs in Part II.

CHAPTER 2
Todi History

The Umbrian-Etruscan Period (1,000 BC–300 BC)

6th-7th BC Cultures (pre-Roman)

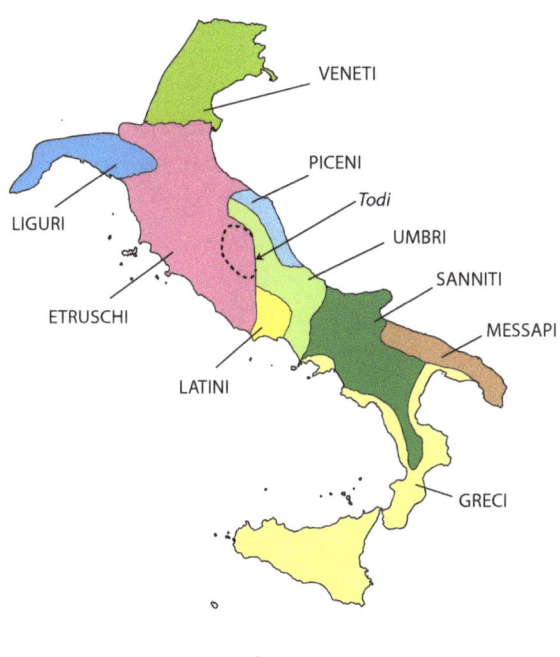

Figure 2. Drawing of Pre-Roman Civilizations throughout Italy

Todi's history extends into prehistoric times, though recorded history only dates back to about 3,000 years ago when the region was occupied by the Umbrians, the oldest known population in Italy.(Fig. 2)

The name Umbri may have derived from the Greek word *imbribus,* meaning "those who survived the flood," though its exact etymology is unknown.

Sometime later, between 9th–8th centuries BC, the Etruscan people began to colonize a large region in central Italy, through Umbria, west to the seacoast, and south to Rome. They likely originated in central Europe during the Bronze Age. Of particular interest is that the Etruscans occupied the land west of the Tiber, whereas the Umbri lived on the eastern side. The vast majority of the remaining Etruscan ruins can be found within a few hours west of Todi. Todi, then, was a town populated by the Umbri on the eastern bank of the Tiber. This may explain the original name *Tutere,* translated from the Etruscan language to mean "border city." The name was subsequently modified by the Romans in Latin to *Tuder,* and finally became Todi in Italian.

Todi had the peculiar distinction of not being conquered by the powerful Etruscans, possibly because of its location and geographic separation. The Umbri were generally not a warring people so the Etruscans were not threatened. Nevertheless, nearly three hundred Umbrian cities went to war against the Etruscans, only to be conquered. Todi remained neutral and peacefully submitted to Etruscan standards.

The city became a place where goods were exchanged and technical knowledge and skills were shared. In addition, the Umbri had access to imported goods from Greece through their historic association with Greek colonizers in southern Italy. Wealthy Etruscans apparently valued such artifacts, and many of their artisans used Greek models in their own craft production.

Remains of the Etruscan era can still be seen.

Porta Marzia, an archway with Etruscan and Roman construction.

Foremost are remnants of the first original walls, built in the 6th–5th centuries BC. The Roman Empire conquest led to complete takeover of the Etruscans, culminating in 280 BC at Vulci, within a two-hour drive from Todi. For the next six centuries, Todi was part of the Roman Empire.

The Roman Period (300 BC–AD 400)

The Romans had a major, long-lasting influence on all areas of life in Todi. The advanced culture incorporated innovations in government, law, engineering, architecture, and urban planning. As the Roman Empire grew, an extensive road system was built. One major route, known as the Flaminia Way, extended from Rome to Ravenna, heading toward central Europe. It ran north at the foot of the Martani mountain range, not far from Todi, along the hill town's eastern side. Undemolished remnants of the road can be visited within a short distance of Todi (see Part IV).

In 98 BC, Emperor Marcus Ulpius Traianus, who came from a Todi family, led the largest-ever expansion of the Roman Empire. Shortly thereafter, in 89 BC, Todi (then called Tuder) was officially given Roman citizenship, a designation that provided its citizens uniquely valued privileges, both civil and military.

By a decree from Emperor Octavius Augustus in 42 BC, Todi became one of the 20 cities in Italy chosen to become a colony for retired veterans of the Roman army. Though the populace of Todi was less than enthusiastic about such a designation, it was apparently considered a small price to pay for an unusual degree of security. At that time, Todi was bestowed with the honorific *Colonia Iulia Fida Tuder* (Todi, a faithful colony).

Over centuries, Todi became a beautiful example of a Roman city. Temples were built on the two highest points that flanked the forum, which covered a series of cisterns that provided a huge water reservoir. A majestic theater was built near the central forum; Roman baths were constructed and an amphitheater was built just outside the city.

The primary north-south road, then known as Cardo Maximus, extended through the city from Porta Fratta (also known as Porta Amerina) to Porta Perugina and saw Roman legions and travelers pass through Todi for hundreds of years.

After the fall of the Roman Empire in AD 476, Todi was overrun in a series of barbarian invasions. Temples of the Roman gods were destroyed, as was the beautiful theater that could be directly accessed from the central forum through the current Piazza Garibaldi. The large amphitheater just outside the city in the area near Porta Romana was also destroyed, as was the Etruscan-Roman necropolis outside Porta Fratta. From the devastation of those dark times, very little remained of the beautiful city, once described as *spendidissima colonia Tuder*.

Nevertheless, what remains today of the Roman era provides a fascinating picture. The central Roman forum still exists, now known as Piazza del Popolo. Around its perimeter sits the imposing medieval cathedral, public buildings, and Renaissance palaces. The Piazza del

Popolo still remains the center of commerce, religion, politics and social life after all these countless centuries.

The concentric ring of Roman walls, partly coincident with the original Etruscan walls can easily be traced in several points around the city and the sites of the Roman gates—Porta Aurea, Porta Catena, Porta di Santa Prassede, Porta Marzia, and Porta Libera.

In addition, impressive engineering feats such as landslide-resistant walls along the sides of the steep, sloping hills and the extensive waterworks all exist as reminders of the splendor of the Roman occupation of Todi. Details of these historic remnants are found in the Points of Interest (POIs) discussed along the tour routes.

Early Middle Ages (6th-11th centuries AD)

This period of history is widely known as the Dark Ages. After the collapse of the Roman Empire, Todi, like the rest of Italy, underwent a period of deep economic, political, and social downturn. Migration of people from various parts of Europe filled the political void left by the centralized Roman government. Todi suffered barbaric invasions by the Goths, Byzantines, and Lombards.

During this time, all the cities in Italy contracted in size. As an example, Rome had been the largest city in Europe in AD 200, with a population of one million. By the sixth century AD, its population had fallen to 30,000! Likewise, Todi shrank significantly.

The fear of aggression and cruelty of the barbarian hordes forced the inhabitants of the cities to seek shelter in the countryside and the woods. Plundered by barbarians, decimated by periodic epidemics and abandoned by its citizens, Todi became a ghost of its former self.

Over the next few centuries, Christianity grew as it offered a modicum of hope for the impoverished people. It was a long, painful growth as many early Church leaders were martyred. Long afterward, these early Church figures were recognized, and many of their relics are housed in the San Fortunato crypt. Around AD 500, Benedict of Norcia (a town two-hours east of Todi) founded the earliest and longest surviving monastic group, known as Benedictines. Their major focus was the study of history and theology. They were responsible for saving many classic texts from destruction.

The Benedictines lived by the principle *ora et labora*—pray and work. Thus, in addition to their organized, ascetic religious life, they began to practice agriculture and its associated activities. They were responsible for land reclamation and drainage, production of baked goods, cheese, and other food staples, wine and beer, and raised sheep and cattle.

High and Late Middle Ages (11th–14th centuries AD)

The low point in history for Todi was the twelfth century AD. During the next two centuries and beyond, remarkable changes occurred throughout Italy. For the next four centuries, Italy's economy and culture grew dramatically and it became the most prominent and successful region in the Western world. Exactly why this happened remains speculative.

Extraordinary development of arts and crafts took place in all areas of economic activity, from agriculture to woodworking; from construction to weaving; from iron and metal processing to tanning of hides. The arts and crafts created a new class of citizens that could rightfully be likened to a new bourgeoisie.

Amidst the tension of emperor-pope alliances and quarrels and under the winds of freedom introduced by enlightened leaders such as Frederick II, Duke of Swabia, Italian cities began to flourish. They were transformed into semi-autonomous city-states, comuni, and began to hum with new energy, creativity, and wealth.

Ultimately, this successful structure laid the groundwork for the Renaissance. City populations began to grow dramatically—Venice, Florence, and Milan each had a population that exceeded 100,000 by the thirteenth century. A mass migration of people from the countryside to the cities occurred after agricultural advances—like crop rotation and technological improvements such as the heavy plow—enhanced farming efficiency and increased crop yields.

Gold coin mintage began in Italy and spread through Europe with a subsequent expansion of commerce. Italian cities became international trading and banking centers, as well as an intellectual crossroads, combining responsive government, Christianity, and the birth of capitalism. Within a hundred years, Italy became the most literate region of the known world. Scholasticism, a philosophy that joined faith with reason, emerged as a dominant belief system. It led to the founding of universities and an embrace of the teachings of theologians like Saint Thomas Aquinas. The paintings of Giotto and the poetry of Dante and Petrarca reflected this new intellectualism. Marco Polo's voyages to China linked the Western world to the East for the first time.

Though Todi remained a small town compared to the great cities of Florence, Bologna, Milan, Genoa, or Venice, in its small way it enjoyed the progress of this era. Todi achieved some notoriety when it joined with Gubbio and Spoleto to support Emperor Frederick as he defeated the Guelphs, who were backed by the nearby cities of Perugia and Orvieto. In AD 1241, the small villages now just inside Porta Romana and Porta Perugina were annexed to Todi, as the final wall of the city enclosed them. This medieval wall remains today as the most prominent feature visible as visitors enter this ancient city.

During the first quarter of the thirteenth century, Saint Francis of Assisi (AD 1181–1226) started a religious movement that has influenced Christianity for centuries, and Umbria became the center of "Franciscanism." Jacopone of Todi followed in his ascetic footsteps and is revered as the most important religious poet of Italy.

Economic progress continued steadily into the fourteenth century. Then, tragically, in the midst of this economic and cultural explosion, *peste bubbonica*—the Black Plague—struck all of Europe. Thirty percent of the entire population was killed during this three-year scourge in the middle of the fourteenth century. Italy did not escape the devastation.

Despite the horrors of those years, the cities immediately began rebuilding. Though a huge segment of the population died, workers were in short supply, so wages increased, raising the standard of living of ordinary citizens.

The Renaissance (15th–17th centuries AD)

Toward the end of the fourteenth century, the comuni continued to thrive as commercial activity created huge wealth. Though raw materials such as wool, silk, wheat, and precious metals were not produced in Italy, they were converted into luxury goods and traded extensively. Bankers and tradesmen became very wealthy and were fond of showcasing their affluence and taste. Great artists and craftsmen were nurtured and encouraged during this time by wealthy patrons, especially in Florence, which became the center of artistic culture.

The flowering of the Renaissance spread quickly among the Italian comuni, from Milan and Venice to Rome and Naples, all of which became wealthier than most cities in Europe.

Like other cities, Todi enjoyed this new era of wealth. City planning and architectural design resulted in significant improvements. Families with great wealth and nobility began building their beautiful palazzi as close to the central piazza as possible to display their wealth and power. During this time, the Consolazione temple was built after the design of Donato Bramante, the architect of some of the most famous buildings in Rome and Milan. This church was widely considered one of the most notable architectural models of the era.

In AD 1566, Angelo Cesi became the bishop of Todi, where he served until his death in 1606. He is credited for his leadership and innovation and is widely considered to be the most influential figure in Todi's history.

Despite the cultural and economic renaissance that swept through Italy, political fighting did not diminish. Bloody disputes occurred between the political powerhouses, the Guelphs and Ghibellines; between families, whose loyalties shifted between the emperor and the pope; and between various alliances of the many city-states. Toward the end of the sixteenth century, Niccolo Macchiavelli, the great historian and social commentator who grew up not far from Todi, expressed his indignation at the political chaos.

Like most Italian cities, Todi survived the political unrest and flourished as a small, rural town for the next few hundred years until it became part of the nation of Italy, officially founded in 1861. Today, Todi sits proudly on a hill high above the verdant valleys of Umbria. More than any other Umbrian city, Todi has treasured its Medieval-Renaissance history, captured in its civic and religious architecture, its road structure that leads upward from beneath the ancient town to the central piazza, and its historic preservation.

Modern Age

The medieval circle of walls continues to insulate the ancient city of Todi from modern development. As one enters Porta Romana, Porta Perugina, or Porta Fratta (a third entrance on the southwest side near the Tempio della Consolazione), virtually no construction later than AD 1700 will be seen. An exception is a modern development just inside the walls from Porta Fratta. To be sure, commercial buildings and businesses have been upgraded over the centuries, but almost all expansion of the city into suburbs has been confined to the hills and valleys outside the old city.

Todi has evolved over the centuries from its historic roots as a commercial and agricultural center. It has become mainly an educational center with classic and scientific lyceums (specialized schools), musical and dramatic performance venues, and a language school.

Populations have come and gone from Todi over three thousand years. Throughout the millennia, this beautiful, ancient city has borne witness to an incredible history. The walking tours we offer you will provide snapshots of this entire span of life in Todi, from the Umbri to the Romans, to the people now known as Italians.

Allow yourself to consider what life must have been like here throughout the ages. Then, when you arrive at the iconic Piazza del Popolo, enjoy a snack—*uno spuntino*—at one of the many *caffè*, while you watch people meander through the plaza.

PART II
Points of Interest (POI)
POI-1. Jacopone da Todi

Jacopo de' Benedetti was born in Todi, in AD 1230, four years after the death of St. Francis, who lived in Assisi, only thirty-five miles to the north. His family was wealthy, and he was sent to Bologna where he was trained as a lawyer. Jacopo returned to Todi and practiced law, dealing with inheritance disputes and property transfers. Though he enjoyed a life of luxury for a time, he became unhappy with himself, his work as a lawyer, and his lifestyle. At age thirty-eight he renounced his affluent lifestyle and family inheritance, and joined the Franciscan Third Order, where he embraced vows of poverty, chastity, and obedience.

For ten years he devoted himself to penance and intense prayer. He began to write poems, known as *laudi*, which could be sung. The *laudi* were written in the vulgar language

Painting of fra Jacopone in prayer by unknown artist of fourteenth century.

(the original Italian language), so the illiterate poor could learn the life and teachings of Christ and the Gospels. At the time, the language of the Catholic Church was Latin, such that ordinary people listened to prayers that they did not understand.

Jacopo became known as Jacopone da Todi as he traveled the countryside as an impoverished missionary, preaching repentance and the love of Christ. At age forty-eight he was admitted as a friar to the Franciscan convent of San Fortunato. There he carried out the most humble duties and devoted his life to meditation, prayer, the study of Scriptures, and poetry. He remained in the convent until age sixty-six.

Some of the *laudi* he wrote were sorrowful lamentations of the state of the Catholic Church, where the papacy pursued goals of political power and wealth, and abandoned the teachings of St. Francis, who stressed spirituality and strict moral rules. A war broke out between the Italian Cardinals Colonna, who rejected the lavish lifestyle of Pope Boniface VIII and his followers. Jacopone continued to be vocal in his opposition to the Pope through his poetry and teachings.

Pope Boniface prevailed, and Cardinals Colonna and others, including Jacopone, were excommunicated. Jacopone was sentenced to prison for life in AD 1298 and was held, wrists and ankles shackled, in an isolated, dark, basement cell in the San Fortunato convent. After five years of solitary confinement, he was released, following the death of Pope Boniface, thanks to the kindness of Pope Benedict XI. He was cared for in the last years of his life by the Poor Clare sisters in the village of Collazzone, near Todi. He died peacefully on Christmas Eve in AD 1306.

During the last eight years of his life, which included the five years of imprisonment and the final three years in the convent of Collazzone, Jacopone reached the peak of his spirituality and his poetry. In AD 1490, a Florentine priest, Francesco Bonnacorsi, one of the first printers in Italy, using the moveable type developed by Johannes Gutenberg, printed the first edition of the ninety-two *laudi* of fra Jacopone.

Bonnacorsi had copied these *laudi* from the manuscripts of fra Jacopone, which are now preserved in the British Museum, where they had been secretly transferred from Italy at the end of the 15th century, to escape censorship during the Catholic Inquisition.

Jacopone's poetry contains an extraordinary richness, in which he expresses tenderness and passion, pain and jubilation, irony, sarcasm, and, most of all, a mystical spirituality. He is considered the greatest Italian poet before Dante and the greatest interpreter of the Franciscan ideal in poetry. His Stabat Mater *laude* has been perfomed by countless famous musicians over the centuries, including Pergolesi, Haydn, Rossini, Liszt, and many others. His *laude*, Donna de Paradiso is considered to be the first text of Italian theater.

POI-2. Teatro Comunale

This theater is the major performance venue in Todi. It was designed by Carlo Gatteschi in 1876 and opened with the operatic performance of Giuseppe Verdi's *Un ballo in maschera* (A Masked Ball). Its interior is elegant and features a beautiful curtain painting that portrays a visit of Ludovico Ariosto, an Italian Renaissance poet, by Annibale Brugnoli.

Décor inside the theater.

The theater, which seats 400, is one of the centers of cultural activity in Todi and the surrounding region. It provides a venue for concerts and theatrical performances year-round and it is also a site used for civic and political meetings.

POI-3. Piazza del Popolo

This central piazza has been the focal point of community activity and commerce for at least 2,500 years. Its symmetric beauty was established during the Roman era, when it was the forum, flanked by majestic temples and public palaces. The piazza can be seen to occupy the space between the two important hills that bracketed the site of Todi's origin.

Looking south from the cathedral steps toward the three administrative buildings.

The original water source which allowed Todi to be built high above the Tiber River was an artesian well discovered by the original inhabitants nearly three thousand years ago. The water, forced up naturally from the aquifer thousands of feet below, provided a permanent water source.

The Romans built massive cisterns in the space between the two hills and then covered it over. Water was directed from la Rocca (the southwest hill) into the cisterns, which also captured rainwater and water that came from other artesian wells in the area. Access to remnants of the cisterns is still possible west of the piazza. The space, once the Roman Forum, is now the Piazza del Popolo. In medieval times, palaces were built along the sides of the piazza. In Roman times, the forum was much larger than the current piazza and reflected the Roman focus on public space.

Open cavernous space, known as the *voltoni*,
on the southeast end of the piazza.

In the thirteenth and fourteenth centuries, public palaces were built along the east and south faces of the piazza, while the cathedral was constructed on the north side during the 12th–13th centuries. Renaissance palaces were built in the 15th–17th centuries on the west side of the piazza by aristocratic families, narrowing the space further.

POI-4. The Cathedral

As you ascend the broad stone staircase to the Duomo, note the impressive central rose window and the two lateral rosettes, as well as the bell tower. The long rectangular façade of the church was built in the eleventh century, and re-built in the fourteenth century after a fire destroyed the early construction. At that time, the bell tower was added and placed asymmetrically, typical of the era. Several other enhancements to the church were made in the sixteenth century.

Todi cathedral located on the north end of
the Piazza del Popolo.

Enter through the impressive wooden door carved by Antonio Bencivenni in 1521. Inside you will be impressed with the harmonious, well-proportioned architecture. The rows of columns on both sides with Corinthian capitals direct your eyes through the central nave toward the sanctuary at the far end. Note that the arches extend across the ceiling past the median, giving a perception of lightness and upward momentum.

Along the right aisle is an additional aisle, like a small side chapel (*navatina*) extending parallel rather than perpendicular, making it a fourth aisle. It was added during the renovations in the fourteenth century. At the entrance of the navatina is a marble baptismal font and over the altar is a painting by Giannicola di Paolo dating from the early sixteenth century. Beautiful stained-glass windows extend down the sides of the church, illustrating various religious themes.

As you arrive at the transept, notice the great suspended crucifix, constructed and suspended in the thirteenth century.

Carlo and Marco Grondona authored a book on the history and art of Todi and describe this part of the church simply and beautifully:

> "The presbytery with its high cross vault, the bare stone walls of the apse, the choir and the altar, form a complex of exquisite harmony, especially towards dusk, when a more intense light ray from the windows transects the great crucifix, while the

rest of the church falls dark and with darkness a deeper silence" (Grondona, p. 146).

In the apse, note the exquisitely carved wooden choir stalls, the work of Antonio and Sebastiano Bencivenni in 1520, truly a masterpiece. Crossing the transept, you will reach the Cesi Chapel, which houses the tombs of Bishop Angelo Cesi as well as his uncle Giovanni Cesi, who preceded him as bishop. The magnificent portraits were painted by Caracci in 1570.

Descending the steps to the crypt, you will see the burial monument of Filippa Uffreduzzi, mother of Angelo Cesi. Just beyond is a recent sculpture (1994) by Fiorenso Bacci representing Saint Martino, born in Todi in the early seventh century, the seventy-fourth pope of the Catholic Church. Descending farther, you will reach a lower-floor crypt— the oldest part of the church, first built in the eighth century—through dark, somewhat eerie corridors, where ancient tombs of bishops and dignitaries are found. Within this crypt are three marble groups depicting religious images. The sculptures were done by Giovanni Pisano in the thirteenth century and had originally been placed on the cathedral façade.

Walking back down the central nave toward the entrance, note the painting Last Judgment beneath the spectacular rose window. The painting was commissioned by Bishop Cesi in 1580. It was painted by il Faenzone, inspired by the famous masterpiece in the Sistine Chapel done twenty-five years earlier by Michaelangelo. Beside the rose window, note the flanking rosettes. One depicts the angel Gabriel, and the other depicts the Virgin Mary. Together they represent the Annunciation of the Virgin Mary, to whom the duomo was dedicated by Pope Boniface VIII around AD 1300.

Rose window with painting of
Last Judgment by il Faenzone.

POI-5. Palazzo Cesi

This massive, lightly colored building is prototypical of the Renaissance palaces. Antonio da Sangallo the Younger was commissioned by the Bishop Angelo Cesi family to build the palace. He had designed the Farnese Palace in Rome and contributed to the design of Saint Peter's in the Vatican.

The Palazzo Cesi shows the typical characteristics of Renaissance palaces. Its façade has a perfectly symmetrical structure and shows the harmony of three— popular among architects of the time. It has three floors and three windows on each floor. The ground floor was used for offices, kitchens, stables and guardrooms. The next floor, known as the *piano nobile* (noble floor) held the dining, reception, entertainment rooms and bedrooms. The top floor was dedicated to staff bedrooms.

According to rules first dictated by Filippo Brunelleschi, the house has a magnificent portal with typical *bugnato* decoration. The name refers to *bugne*, large stones that partly project outward from the wall and are sometimes used at the corners of the building.

The windows are square on the lowest and highest floors, and rectangular on the middle floor, accentuating the vertical dimension. Moreover, the stone relief over the middle floor windows is meant to lighten the visual impact.

∼

Palace of Bishop Cesi adjacent to the cathedral.

The façade is stucco over brick instead of stone, creating a smooth surface, which, along with the other features described, set a new standard for elegance. The roof is flat with wide overhanging eaves and decorative brackets beneath them, typical Renaissance palace characteristics. Typical as well is an internal courtyard, colonnaded along its perimeter, with a wide, beautiful staircase to access the upper two floors.

POI-6. Angelo Cesi

Angelo Cesi was born in Rome in AD 1530, the son of Chiappino and Filippa Uffreduzzi, a noble family from Todi. Angelo was elected bishop at age 36 and died in Todi in 1606 after serving as its bishop for forty years.

Portrait of Angelo Cesi painted by Carracci.

Angelo Cesi became a bishop shortly after the Council of Trent. He witnessed the conflict of approach to religion that was prevalent at the time. He had frequent and friendly relationships with two important clerics, Filippo Neri and Carlo Borromeo.

Filippo Neri, sometimes called the "third apostle of Rome," after Saint Peter and Saint Paul, was the prototype of the poor priest. He had an open and jovial personality and was able to live and work with the poor and play happily with the children. Carlo Borromeo was bishop of Milan. He had a severe and uncompromising character, both within himself and with others. He was an intransigent guardian of Catholic orthodoxy. He renounced his wealth and gave all his property to the Church and to the poor of Milan, an example that Bishop Cesi followed closely.

Bishop Cesi ordered the remains of Jacopone. who had been excommunicated by Pope Boniface VIII, transferred to the Church of San Fortunato for burial, thereby restoring his dignity and honor. Jacopone's reputation, thanks to Bishop Cesi's decision, led to a profound recognition of the spirituality of the great poet.

Over the four decades of his leadership, Bishop Cesi dedicated all his wealth to improve the urban face of Todi. He personally financed construction of the Bishop's Palace. He oversaw construction of the via Cesia, a very practical idea which linked the entrance to Todi at Porta Perugina with Porta Romana. He supported construction of Tempio della Consolazione and Tempio Crocifisso to provide symmetrical churches at the two southern entrances to Todi. He also oversaw construction of the Fonte della Rua (sometimes called Fonte Cesia) and other architectural projects, including works in the cathedral: the painting of Last Judgment and the Cesi Chapel.

Despite his aristocratic roots, Bishop Cesi was

respectful of the Franciscan and Jacopone emphasis on serving the poor. To that end, he used his authority to coerce priests, who were accustomed to the good life in the shadow of the Bishop's Palace, to populate countryside parishes where they could share the lives and struggles of the poor.

The tomb of Angelo Cesi and a magnificent portrait of him by the artist Caracci can be found in the Cesi Chapel in the cathedral.

POI-7. Bishop's Palace

Commissioned by Angelo Cesi and designed by the Milan architect Domenico Bianchi, the palace was completed in AD 1593. It has a gallery adorned with frescos by Andrea Polinori as well as an extensive representation of the entire Diocese of Todi, including all the roads, villages and castles that existed in the sixteenth century. The historic archives stored here date back to the twelfth century. They offer one of the oldest, most detailed and reliable sources of Todi's life from the Middle Ages to today.

∽

Gallery of the Bishop's Palace showing beautiful frescoes by Andrea Polinori

The Throne Room was frescoed by Ferrau da Faenza (il Faenzone) in 1594 and includes portraits of the bishops that served Todi over the centuries.

The view from the windows of the top floor that overlook Todi and the surrounding countryside is simply spectacular.

POI-8. Renaissance Palaces and Lordships

Along the sides of the Piazza del Popolo, wealthy families built their palazzi in the most prominent location in Todi; namely, facing the very center of town. They were constructed in the sixteenth century, a time when the most famous architects in Italian history—such as Bramante, Peruzzi, Antonio da Sangallo the Younger, and Vignola—were consulted for their beautiful designs. During the Renaissance, architecture was considered a great form of art, and beauty was manifested in the harmony of simple mathematical and geometric principles, symmetrical and balanced forms based on squares, circles and triangles.

Throughout the center of Todi and scattered elsewhere, one can see a number of Renaissance palaces. They are easily recognizable by several characteristic features. They often have portals with bugnato. This is sometimes also seen on the building corners in the larger palaces. They commonly have overhanging eaves with decorative brackets beneath them. The internal courtyards and large staircases are often colonnaded.

Some of the more important historic palaces in Todi have plaques with the name of the family that built them and the century in which they were built.

POI-9. Palazzo del Capitano del Popolo

This palazzo, the Palace of the Captain of the People, was built immediately next to the Palazzo del Popolo around AD 1290, and in later years the two were connected. It is one of three public buildings where the judicial and other administrative offices of Todi have existed for seven hundred years. The open covered area on the ground floor, built on large columns and vaults—*voltoni*—was apparently occupied by the city's crossbowmen during the Middle Ages.

Photograph of the two administrative buildings on the southeast end of Piazza del Popolo: Palazzo del Capitano (left) and Palazzo del Popolo (right)

The floor façade above the voltoni features three *trifore,* popular mullioned triple windows. Each component is separated by columned designs and frames with cuspate ornamentation of leaves, a symbolic representation of the local hilly landscape covered by trees. Four somewhat less ornate trifore are visible on the top floor. Note also the decorative coats of arms on the façade, representing wealthy families of Todi, as well as the small bell, which was rung to call citizens to the central piazza for important announcements.

POI-10. Palazzo del Popolo

As you face the Palazzo del Capitano, the attached building on the right, fronted by a large stone staircase, is the Palace of the People. It was built between AD 1210 and 1220 and is one of the earliest public buildings of the era in all of Italy. Originally, the front of the building was its south face. As you walk along the side, you will be on Piazza Garibaldi. From there, as you face the palace, you can see the outline of the original staircase, bricked in when the front entrance was moved in 1270. Above a bricked-in door there is a stone eagle, one of the oldest versions of Todi's symbol.

A community bell tower was added in AD 1523, the official way for the common people to tell time before a clock was installed at a later date.

As you return to the current entrance, at the top of the staircase a door allows access to a large, stone hall—Sala delle Pietre, still in use today for special exhibits and conferences. On the side of the door, outside, fixed in the wall are standard measures of length, in iron. Strangely enough, each of the comuni had their own official measures and standards!

This second of the three municipal buildings, which was built before the other two, has been the seat of governance for eight centuries. In the Middle Ages, Todi was ruled by the *podesta*—a leader who was chosen by the aristocracy and served a one-year term—and a Municipal Council. Today the mayor's office and the town council are still present in this building.

Beneath the Palace of the Captain and the Palace of

the People are the buried remains of the Roman cisterns used to store water for citizens of Todi dating back over two thousand years.

POI-11. Mars Statue

In 1835, this bronze, nearly life-size statue was unearthed on the hill below Montesanto, west of Todi. It had been buried since the fourth or fifth century BC. The statue is a classic representation of an Etruscan soldier and has an inscription carved into it in the extinct Umbrian language using Etruscan characters.

Points of Interest (POI)

Full-scale replica of Mars statue.

This statue is typical of a number of bronze sculptures that were made at the time by the Etruscans, possibly near the nearby town of Orvieto. It was likely buried ritually as an offering to the gods. The original statue resides in the Museo Gregoriano in the Vatican. An exact replica can be seen in Todi, at the museum in the Palazzo del Popolo, open to the public.

This unique finding adds to our understanding of the integral relationship between the Umbrian inhabitants of Todi and their Etruscan neighbors, dating back over 2,500 years.

POI-12. Palazzo dei Priori

The third public building, directly facing the cathedral, is the Palazzo dei Priori—Palace of Priors. *Priori* is derived from Latin, meaning prominent. It was built in AD 1330 as a place where important community representatives of art and crafts met. Shortly after it was constructed, legislative activity began to develop here in concert with the two previously mentioned municipal buildings.

The palace windows with their stone frames are elegant in their simplicity. The palace tower with its trapezoidal section demonstrates power as well as elegance and was meant to somewhat balance the cathedral bell tower on the north end of the piazza. Above the top floor windows is a bronze eagle, Todi's symbol, that was installed about AD 1340. The two baby eagles on its wings represented the cities of Amelia and Terni, which were under the domination of Todi at the time.

POI-13. Eagle's Nest Legend

The origin of Todi as a town dates somewhere between the 9th to 10th centuries BC. According to legend, the Umbrians desired to build a town on the western shore of the Tiber. A group of men had begun to assemble stone walls along the river bank to surround the new town when they stopped to eat lunch, which was spread on a large cloth.

Suddenly, an eagle swooped down and snatched the cloth in its talons, flew away and deposited it on the top of the hill, nearly 1,000 feet above the shore, on the eastern side. The workers felt it was a message from the gods and concurred that a more appropriate site for the new town would be at the top of the hill.

The legend has persisted for centuries and accounts for the fact that the symbol of Todi continues to be an eagle with outstretched wings, holding a cloth in its claws.

POI-14. Piazza Garibaldi

This small, charming square dates back to Roman times. Two thousand years ago, it provided access to a beautiful Roman theater.

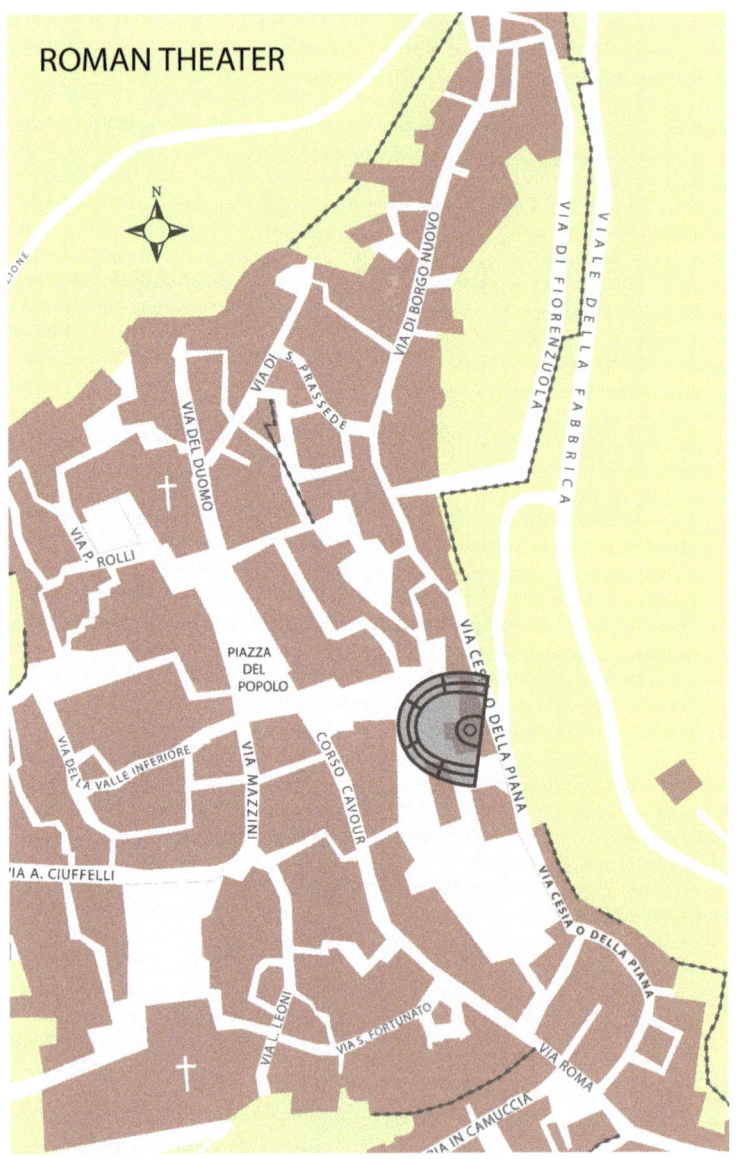

Figure 3. Sketch of the likely site of a Roman theater.

Today the main feature of this historic spot is a statue commemorating Giuseppe Garibaldi, who played a major role in the ultimate unification of Italy that occurred in 1861.

Garibaldi was a revolutionary most of his adult life; first in South America, then back in Italy where he dedicated himself to its unification. He was respected as an honest man, revered by ordinary people and known widely for his bravery.

On one of his forays in 1859, as he escaped from Rome and was chased by the French, he passed through Todi, where he was hailed as a folk hero. A cypress tree was planted in his honor at that time and remains to this day.

Piazza Garibaldi looking east.

Behind the cypress tree is a Renaissance palazzo

commissioned by Viviano Atti in 1552. Enjoy the incomparable view of the valley to the east of Todi from the Piazza Garibaldi. One can easily imagine the strategic defensive choice of this high hill by Todi's founders and inhabitants over the centuries.

POI-15. San Fortunato Church

The church of Saint Fortunato was built on the site of a Roman temple, on the highest point in Todi. It stands 1,350 feet above sea level and 800 feet above the Tiber River. The original church was built by the Benedictines as part of their monastery in the twelfth century AD. It was consecrated by Pope Innocent III in 1198. Two stone lions flank the steps and possibly date as far back as the seventh century.

In AD 1292, the Franciscans acquired the church and rebuilt it as one of the first "hall churches," very long and tall, yet somewhat wide, and characteristically much brighter than similar churches in France and elsewhere. Construction began, but was stopped in 1348 when the plague decimated the populace of Todi. Work was restarted and interrupted at times due to political conflicts. By 1465, the church was almost completed, and to this day it has never been fully completed. Among the Franciscan churches, San Fortunato is second only to the Basilica in Assisi in size.

Façade of San Fortunato.
Note that the upper section was never completed.

An imposing stone staircase rises to the front of the church, interspersed with simple grass landscaping. Looking at the front, it is obvious that the upper half of the façade was never completed due to lack of funds. Nevertheless, the lower façade, designed by Giovanni di Santuccio in 1420, was constructed over a period of forty years. Three portals are present, each with five spiraling pilasters surrounding it. All are decorated with leaves and animals and flanked by sculptures depicting saints and apostles.

Close-up of the ornate entrance to San Fortunato.

Upon entry, one is struck by the high, majestic nave supported by pillars that lead to a vaulted ceiling. The side altars are recessed to emphasize the building's height. The church is unusually bright, with high lancet windows along the sides and three large windows over the sanctuary at the far end. The front windows are small, likely because the upper façade was never completed.

Frescoes can be seen along the sides, most only partially remaining. In the fourth chapel on the right is a famous fresco, Madonna and Child with Angels, painted by Masolino da Panicale in 1432.

Madonna with Child painted
by Masolino da Panicale.

The altar is surrounded by ten supporting columns, topped by delicate rosettes. Between the columns are paintings of saints done by I. Sabatini in 1861. A statue of Saint Fortunato stands at the top of the altar, completed in 1643.

On the right side of the apse, high on the wall, a stone pulpit can be seen, typically Franciscan, where preaching to very large crowds of people was emphasized. Another wooden pulpit can be seen high on the same wall. Most impressive are the fifty-eight walnut choir stalls, carved in 1590 by Antonio Maffei from Gubbio. Inlaid in the center of each is the town symbol, the eagle.

A crypt can be found below the sanctuary. The remains of Saint Fortunato are present in a sarcophagus. His burial was commissioned by Bishop Cesi in 1598, along with the remains of Saint Callisto, Saint Cassiano, Saint Romana, and Saint Degna, as well as the blessed fra Jacopone.

Accessed from the inside, on the far left end of the church is an impressive bell tower, built in AD 1460, which is open to the public. Its 360-degree views of Todi and its surroundings are spectacular.

POI-16. Jacopone da Todi Lyceum

A lyceum (*liceo*) is a secondary-level school that offers preparation for students who want to pursue university-level academic training. It is equivalent to a prestigious high school in the United States. Students in Todi can pursue classical and scientific training at this school, which serves an extensive geographic region around Todi.

The historical significance of the school is that it occupies most of the old monastery of Franciscan friars. This complex, including the Church of Saint Fortunato with its gigantic bell tower, was built in the 14th–15th centuries. It stood as the Franciscan complex second only to the monastery and basilica of St. Francis in Assisi.

Moreover, this monastery was the place where fra Jacopone, one of the two greatest sons of Todi, was first accepted as a minor friar in the Franciscan order. He spent five painful years incarcerated in the quarters beneath the monastery when Pope Boniface VIII excommunicated him and had him imprisoned.

Galleries of the lyceum, formerly a monastery.

The complex has many structural attributes, including the simple cloister, the inside architecture, the famous adjacent church, and even the beautiful archives and public library of Todi that were once part of this Franciscan complex.

POI-17. La Rocca and San Callisto Cistern

Beside the friary of San Fortunato is a stone structure. It is the San Callisto cistern, which dates back to Roman times. According to legend, Saint Cassiano was incarcerated and died in AD 304 in this small building that had been converted to a prison.

Walking west through the Rocca, you will see the remains of a line of walls. At the far end stands a tower, il Mastio. This wall structure was commissioned by Pope Gregory XI and built in AD 1373 over the ruins of the Abbey of Saint Leucio. The wall was constructed to assure loyalty to the pope during the ongoing feud between the Guelphs and Ghibbelines. The pope was determined to maintain strict control over the often-rebellious citizens of Todi.

Tower at the west end of the Piazzale della Rocca with remnants of fortress wall (il Mastio)

Less than two centuries later, la Rocca was razed and its massive stones were used for the construction of the Tempio della Conolazione.

Near the tower, one is struck by the four steel pillars that stand thirteen meters in height. These pillars were first constructed in 1979 by a famous American sculptor, Beverly Pepper. The city of Todi commissioned the art piece, and the four columns stood as an exhibit in the Piazza del Popolo.

Sometime later the sculptures were removed and shown in a number of exhibitions around the world. Ms. Pepper, who was born in Brooklyn in 1922, lived outside of Todi for nearly fifty years. In 2019 she donated twenty metal sculptures to Todi, including the original four pillars. This donation resulted in creation of the Beverly Pepper Sculpture Garden, inaugurated by the city of Todi.

The sculptures, along with strategically placed metal benches carved from Pietra serena, a stone found near Lake Trasimeno, were erected permanently along a wooded path that extends from la Rocca downward to the Tempio della Consolazione (see **POI-29**). The sculpture garden magically links la Rocca, the original site of Umbri colonization, to the Tempio, which was completed during the glorious days of the Renaissance.

POI-18. The Medieval Walls and Gates

The historical urban evolution of Todi is exemplified by three concentric circles of walls. The highest, first circle is of Etruscan and Roman origin, dating between the fourth to the second centuries BC. As the city grew, a second, lower circle was constructed by the Romans in the second century AD. About a thousand years later, the third—and final—set of walls was built in the thirteenth century.

Porta fratta, the oldest entrance to Todi,
after reconstruction. Medieval walls connecting
the entryway are original.

All three sets of walls were constructed using massive stones, cut and shaped from a quarry over twenty miles from Todi. They were likely transported by a conveyor made of logs, pulled along by human power. How they were dragged up the steep hill remains a mystery. Given the enormity of the project, it comes as no surprise that stone from the earlier walls was used to help build the subsequent two circles. Nor is it surprising that the original stones were used centuries later to aid in the construction of Christian churches and medieval palaces, a historical fact throughout Italy.

The original Etruscan walls were built with rectangular stone blocks without mortar. Though the Etruscans had no formal knowledge of physics, they were able to create stable and permanent walls. In addition, they are credited with developing the principle of the arch, which they used at entry points. As far back as 300 BC, the Romans developed cutting techniques to make the granite blocks very similar in size. In later centuries, the Romans improved construction techniques with the development of mortar, kiln-dried bricks, and unique geometric construction that they applied to temples and other buildings.

Other engineering advances made by the Romans include construction of sustaining walls to prevent erosion and landslides. Two major examples are the wall on the west side of the city, just below via Termoli outside the city, very close to the Porta Orvietana parking area; and the Nicchioni (see POI-26) on the east side. These walls have stood for over two thousand years.

Deteriorating remains of an early portal
(Porta Orvietana) along original medieval wall.

The walls had important functions. First, they offered security from invasion by armies and robbers. It is notable that in Todi's long history, the walls were never breached by invaders. The third set of walls afforded security as they wrapped around the small villages, such as Borgo Nuovo, that became incorporated into Todi in the thirteenth century.

The gates were the only portals of entry into Todi. They were thick and strong, made of iron and wood, and were closed every night. During the day, they were opened and served to allow passage in and out and to collect taxes and duties (*gabelle*). There is little remaining of the first set of walls, though they are easily visible in certain places as mentioned in Tours 2, 3 and 4.

A road, about five kilometers long, skirts the entire circumference of the lowest set of walls. Notably, almost no construction within the walls occurred after the 17th century. Except for one exception (**see POI-28**). Since then, all new development has been done on the hillsides outside the walls, thus preserving the historic character of the town.

POI-19. Porta Perugina and Borgo Nuovo

Borgo Nuovo developed as a small village located outside the urban limits of the Roman Tuder. As the town grew, it began to encroach on the small villages that had grown up at the feet of Todi. When the final set of protective walls was completed, it embraced Borgo Nuovo, which became annexed to Todi. The northern entrance to Todi, Porta Perugina, passes through the Borgo and leads up the hill to the central piazza.

View of Porta Perugina from outside the walls.

Porta Perugina appears today as a series of overlapping arches, creating a change from the original structure from the thirteenth century. The change was made in the sixteenth century to strengthen the portal, and a powerful *bastione* (rampart) was built, seen on the left of the gate from the outside, and a *torrione* (tower) on the right. The bastione is now a small park with stunning views to the north and east.

POI-20. The Agricultural High School

A narrow, tree-lined road, the Viale Montecristo, leads to the Istituto Tecnico Agrario, a prestigious High School of Agriculture, founded in 1864. The school buildings had been the Monastery of Montecristo, founded in the 1200s by the Benedictines. In 1248, it became a monastery for the Sisters of Saint Clare.

Visitors are welcome to tour the Istituto with prior reservations. Characteristics of the original Medieval monastery can be seen there, which have been renovated a number of times over the centuries. Other interesting features include a museum of biodiversity, a modern wine cellar, and an experimental garden of aromatic herbs. A small shop offers a number of items for purchase, including locally harvested fruits and vegetables, extra-virgin olive oil, wine, and a variety of cheeses from cows, sheep, and goats.

Thanks to enlightened leadership, the Istituto has become a model for teaching and development of technology that supports "farm to table" concepts.

POI-21. Medieval Houses and Neighborhood

When the final circumferential wall was constructed in the thirteenth century, enclosing the villages at the base of the city, no further demolition and reconstruction of any magnitude occurred. Today, Todi mostly embodies the architecture and structure developed in the Middle Ages and Renaissance, preserved better than any place in Italy.

Medieval houses line the streets and are present in every quarter of the city. During the Renaissance, some of the buildings were incorporated into grand palaces or mansions, constructed by wealthy landowners who desired an urban home. Not surprisingly, their palazzi were built around the Piazza del Popolo, the center of activity within the city.

Typical medieval houses along the streets were

arranged *a striscia*, meaning that all entrances abutted the street in a line. Two front doors were typical. The first was about six feet wide and sited at the street level. A second door, about 2-1/2 feet wide was raised above the street level and accessed by a step. The larger door provided access to a business, a work space, or a stable for animals. The smaller entrance opened to a staircase to the first floor (second level), where a kitchen and bedrooms were located. Sometimes a ladder led to a second floor. More well-to-do families may have had two large doors as well as the small door. Along the city district of via di Borgo Nuovo one can find among the best preserved examples of Medieval city structure and organization in Italy.

Families typically tended a small garden in the back for cultivation of vegetables and breeding of chickens and rabbits for food.

Typical neighborhood with small, shared piazza for communal use.

The medieval doors often had handsome door jambs and arches made from travertine, a white limestone common in Italy. Even doors that have been bricked over through the centuries retain beautiful outlines of travertine arches.

The narrow streets invited socialization. In the evening, families would bring chairs and sit, children playing, women embroidering, and parents and grandparents talking and watching over their children. Such experiences still exist in some parts of the city. Television and social media, as well as movement of families away from the old city, have resulted in streets that are silent in the late evenings after traffic and commerce have faded away at day's end. Though Todi has shrunk in size like many similar Italian cities, some resurgence of the old ways has come from settlement by a new wave of immigrants. So, throughout the centuries, life has waxed and waned, but the old city has remained a permanent place for many hundreds of years.

POI-22. Monastery of the Poor Clares and the Purgatorio Painting

This small monastery is owned by The Sisters of Saint Clare who purchased it in AD 1600 from the Servite monastic order. The Servites were founded in AD 1245 and during the same century added the monastery in Todi. Their general, or leader, was Filippo Benizi, who entered the Order in 1254, and died in Todi thirty years later. He was venerated by the citizens of Todi, who commissioned a fresco to be painted in his honor in the monastery.

The fresco occupies a choir wall in the inner chapel and can only be seen by appointment. Of note, when the Poor Clares bought the monastery in 1600, the fresco was plastered over. It was not discovered until 1974, when maintenance work occurred, and has been subsequently restored.

The Purgatorio painting by an unknown Umbrian
artist of the fourteenth century

The painting, which is probably the first iconographic representation of Purgatory, only a few decades later than Dante's Divine Comedy, is a masterpiece of Umbrian painting of the fourteenth century. It depicts the passing of souls from Purgatory to Paradise through the merits of Christ and with the intercession of the Virgin Mary, along with the blessed Filippo Benizi in a reception by Saint Peter.

The painting is based on "Saint Patrick's Purgatory," a legend well known in the Middle Ages. In the fresco,

Saint Patrick is dressed in the luxurious vestments of a bishop. Purgatory is depicted as a section of an enormous mountain, in which there are seven caverns, representing the seven capital sins.

The artist of the fresco is unknown, but was likely a disciple of the school of Jacopo di Mino del Pellicciaio. Several paintings in the San Fortunato church are similarly attributed to this artist. Filippo Benizi was sanctified in AD 1671. He died in this monastery and his cell was converted into a chapel. Benizi was a contemporary of fra Jacopone and followed the same vows of poverty and humility.

POI-23. Waterworks and Fonte Scannabecco

Over the centuries, the inhabitants of Todi remained aware of the importance of a water supply for their town. Ductwork was expanded to meet the needs of a growing population. Between the thirteenth and fourteenth centuries AD, Todi had grown to 12,000 residents. For reference, the old city today has 7,000 inhabitants.

During this warring period, horses became ever more important in the formation of protective armies. In fact, at one time every family was expected to keep a horse for such use. (There is historical documentation of a time that Todi provided 1,000 horsemen to accompany Pope Boniface VIII from Todi to Rome!)

In 1241, the *podesta* (mayor) of Todi, Scannabecco of Bologna, constructed the Fonte Scannabecco. It was one of many distributed throughout the town and remains as a splendid artistic example of the importance of water to the community. The *fonte* has three sections, each somewhat lower than the former. The highest section received fresh water and was used for drinking water for the residents and their horses. The middle section provided water to carry home for washing clothes and dishes. The lowest section was used for washing clothes at the fountain.

Scannabecco fountain with decorative arches and levels descending from left to right.

It is worth noting that the average consumption of water by a horse is thirty to sixty liters per day. Considering the number of horses in Todi during the twelfth and thirteenth centuries, up to 75,000 liters per day would be required!

Each of the three pools is covered by a portico with carved capitals. Eight elegant arches add architectural beauty to the fountain.

POI-24. Palazzo Pongelli

This beautiful palace is located about halfway along via Cesia o della Piana. Palazzo Pongelli was built in a classic Renaissance style and is characterized by a splendid loggia and a hanging garden, which overlooks the hills, valleys and mountains east of Todi. It is one of the best-preserved Renaissance buildings in Todi and can be toured by appointment. The rooms of the second (noble) floor have beautiful painted ceilings, decorated walls, doors with friezes and lined arches and exceptional furnishings. In one of the noble floor rooms, a series of seventeenth-century paintings can be seen, which depict the life and legend of fra Jacopone. The paintings were done by several artists working in Todi at the time, including Polinori, Sensini and others.

Prominent palazzo with adjacent hanging gardens.

Standing near the hanging gardens in the loggia, one can appreciate the opulence of the wealthy noblemen who have lived there over the centuries. The current owner, Count Eugerio Maria Pongelli, is an affable, welcoming host.

POI-25. Sant' Ilario

This simple, unassuming church was the first church built in Todi. Its original name was the Church of Saint Ilario. In an archive of Saint Prassede, the origin of the church is paraphrased as follows:

The Church of Saint Ilario was built in the year AD 301 during the Roman era by Bishop Cassiano. In the Episcopal Synod year of AD 1373, the church was said to be referred to as Todi's cathedral— as far back as AD 303.

It was re-consecrated in 1249 and again in 1623 when it received its current name, San Carlo.

Small, ancient church with simple façade and unique bell tower.

The church has been lovingly restored over the past few years. It is characterized by an extremely elegant, yet simple façade. Most notable is the prominent triple set of bells at the top. The inside of the church is characterized by a long, single nave, with minimal ornamentation, a testimony to its medieval construction.

POI-26. Nicchioni and Roman Sustaining Structures

Built on a steep hill, Todi has been at risk of earth slides over many centuries, especially as the town began expanding outward, since downward expansion was limited by the defensive walls. These four niches, or *nicchioni,* constructed in the Roman era, are architecturally interesting. Though beautiful in their simplicity, they are largely unadorned. Given the location and their simplicity, it is unlikely they were part of a temple or other important public structure.

Arches date to Roman times, probably built to support massive sustaining walls.

In fact, they are likely structural devices to bear the weight of building expansion above them. The Roman engineering sophistication cannot be overstated.

Walking around the perimeter of the town, one can see examples of erosion prevention along the walls, wherein the stonework is constructed with an inward angle as it rises from the ground. The fact that these walls have stood for many centuries is testimony to the quality of construction.

POI-27. The Roman Amphitheater and the churches of San Filippo and San Nicolò

From a historical point of view, the area just inside the Porta Romana has considerable interest. On the right side stands the hospital of St. Nicolò, built in the mid-fourteenth century. Next to it stands the church of Saint Filippo Benizi, commissioned by Bishop Angelo Cesi in the sixteenth century. It contains a marble statue of Saint Filippo, possibly done by the famous sculptor Lorenzo Bernini. The bones of Saint Filippo rest in an urn beneath the altar.

On the left side of via Matteotti is the Largo Ulpio Traiano, the churchyard of San Nicolò, or Saint Nicholas. The name Ulpio Traiano refers to the traditional belief that the origin of Emperor Marcus Ulpius Traianus was the Ulpia family from Tuder. Until the mid-1800s, the main street to the central piazza was known as via Ulpiana. Thereafter, the road was named in three separate parts: via Matteotti, via Roma and via Cavour.

In this *largo* (meaning small place), you can see the simple, yet elegant, façade of San Nicolò de Criptis, a church built on the site of a Roman amphitheater.

Points of Interest (POI)

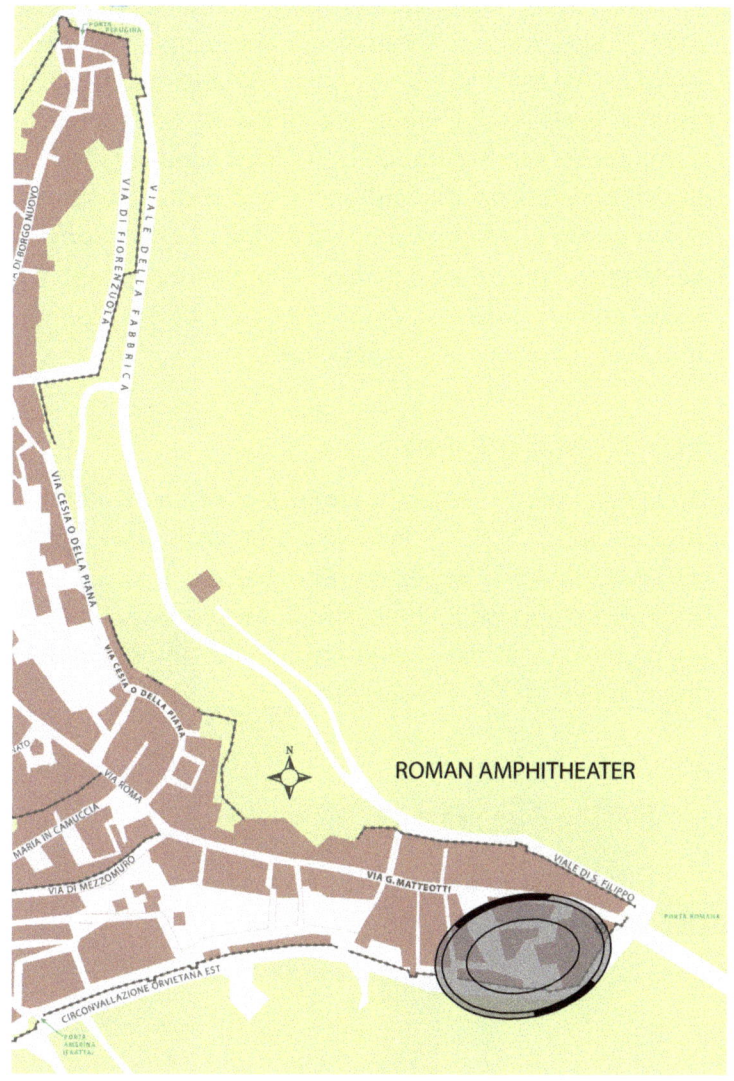

Figure 4. Sketch of the likely site of
a Roman amphitheater

The church, San Nicolò de Criptis, meaning "of the caves," likely refers to the presence of nearby catacombs. It was first constructed in AD 1095 and its remains can be seen in the space occupied by the original amphitheater. A second church, San Nicolò, was built in the mid-fourteenth century. It reshaped the area as it was constructed perpendicular to the original church, an unusual way to site a church. A number of paintings from both these historic churches have been removed to the city's museum for preservation.

POI-28. Mezzomuro

This long street proceeds along the ramparts of the Roman wall. It is obvious that this high, steep wall allowed for nearly impenetrable defense of the city. The view down the valley from this vantage point allowed the defenders of the walled city to see adversaries for many miles.

View of the valley south of Todi from the walkway along the base of original Roman walls.

Below the street is the only area in the ancient city where "suburbs" have been built within the last several decades, inside the medieval walls.

POI-29. Tempio della Consolazione

The formal name for the church is Tempio di Santa Maria della Consolazione, or the church of Saint Mary of Consolation. Construction began in AD 1508 at the site of a supposed miracle. According to legend, a workman had cleaned an image of the Virgin Mary that had been located at the site. He wiped his blind eye with the cloth and his sight was restored. The church was built on the site and the altar currently houses the Virgin Mary image.

This church is unique as a Renaissance work of art as it

stands alone just outside the city walls. Most Renaissance churches had an elongated shape or were built in the form of the Latin cross. Tempio della Consolazione has a unique shape. It is perfectly symmetrical in the form of a Greek cross. This architectural style was introduced by Donato Bramante, whose early design of Saint Peter's Basilica in the Vatican was similarly structured, though ultimately the structure of Saint Peter's was modified under the supervision of other prominent architects, including Michelangelo.

Frontal view of the Tempio della Consolazione.

Thus, the design of Tempio della Consolazione may not have been done personally by Bramante, but it was drawn by students influenced by him. At least four architects had a hand in the construction, which was not completed until 1607, a full century after it was started.

From the outside, the symmetry is obvious with one exception. Three of the apses are polygonal, but the north-facing apse is semi-circular. The reason for this remains unknown. Each apse is capped with a semi-spherical dome. Atop the apses is a square balcony that surrounds the church, within which rises a stately, though simple elliptical dome.

Its structure demonstrates the value placed by Renaissance architects on basic geometric principles. The apses appear from a distance in a semi-circular style. The center of the church is a perfect square with pillars in the four corners. The windows walls, structural, and artistic features are all symmetrical. Thus, the use of squares, circles, triangles and polygons all contribute to the simple, elegant beauty. The genius of the Bramante school is that this building was completed over one hundred years and always remained true to the original design.

Inside the church, geometric symmetry was used to tell the New Testament story. Each of the three polygonal apses has four niches, so that all twelve Apostles are represented. In the very center, according to the original design, the plan was for placement of statues of the Virgin Mary and the child Jesus. In the four corners were sited statues of the four Evangelists. At the apex of the dome a dove was painted, representing the Holy Spirit. Thus, architectural features were drawn purposely to fulfill a theological intent.

Without question, the Tempio della Consolazione is one of the most unique Renaissance churches in all Italy. Look at it from a distance as it stands alone. Its solitary placement reflects permanence, elegant in its simplicity.

POI-30. The Church of Santa Maria in Camuccia

This church was built on the site of a Roman temple dedicated to Venus Aurea. The name *aurea* means golden, or splendid. With the rise of Christianity, using some stone from the original temple, the church was built to honor the Virgin Mary, who also received the accolade "golden," referring to her wisdom and love. The origin and meaning of the word *Camuccia* is unknown.

Remains of the original eighth-century church as well as archeological findings of Roman origin can be seen on the lower floor of the church. The building is square-shaped and has an elegant portal with two columns with Corinthian capitals, deriving from the Roman temple.

∼

Façade of the church structure that dates back to
the eighth century AD

Inside the church are a number of interesting paintings. One unique work of art is a twelfth-century wooden sculpture of the enthroned Madonna, the *sedes sapientiae* (seat of wisdom). For security reasons, it is now housed in the crypt of the cathedral. It is very similar to a statue found in Collazzone, a village about ten miles from Todi. A near-identical wood sculpture was also found in a small Tuscan town, Sansepolcro. This statue is now housed in the Berlin Art Museum.

∼

Famous wooden statue that originally stood in the church. Now resides in the crypt of the cathedral.

From the twelfth to nineteenth centuries, a Benedictine abbey was associated with the church. It is likely that fra Jacopone was hosted at the church at various times.

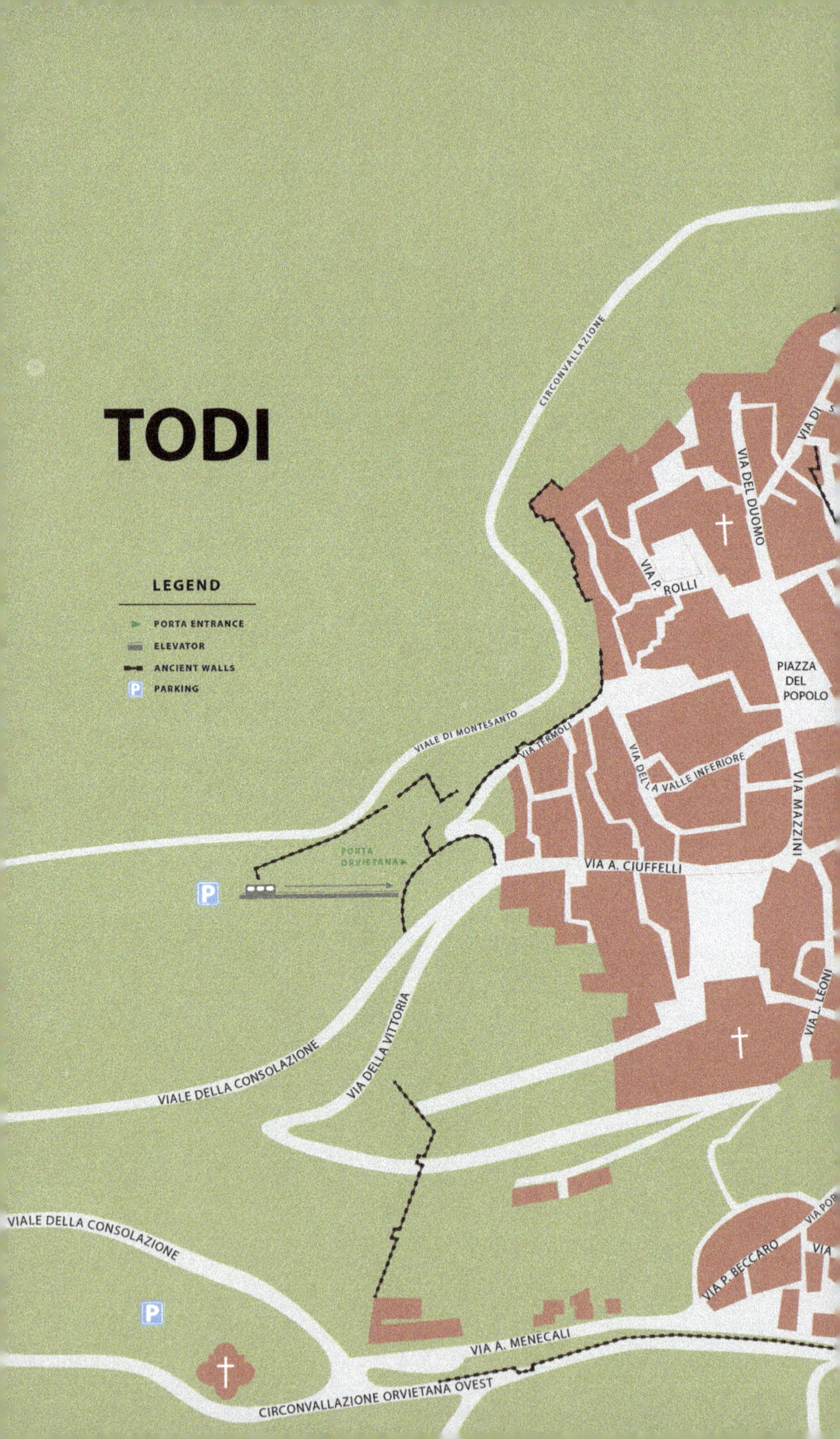

TODI

LEGEND
- ▶ PORTA ENTRANCE
- ▬ ELEVATOR
- ▬▬ ANCIENT WALLS
- 🅿 PARKING

CIRCONVALLAZIONE

VIA DEL DUOMO

VIA DI S.

VIA P. ROLLI

PIAZZA DEL POPOLO

VIALE DI MONTESANTO

VIA TERZOLI

VIA DELLA VALLE INFERIORE

VIA MAZZINI

PORTA ORVIETANA

VIA A. CIUFFELLI

VIA T. LEONI

VIALE DELLA CONSOLAZIONE

VIA DELLA VITTORIA

VIALE DELLA CONSOLAZIONE

VIA P. BECCARO

VIA POR

VIA

VIA A. MENECALI

CIRCONVALLAZIONE ORVIETANA OVEST

PART III
Walking Tours

Introduction

One of the unique features of Todi is its pyramidal shape. At the base of the ancient town, the medieval walls are visible along the road that runs beside them. As mentioned previously, three main roads lead from the base of the city up to the main square—Piazza del Popolo. We have provided four major tour routes.

Tour Route 1 is dedicated to the fascinating historic sites surrounding the central square, the Piazza del Popolo and the Church of San Fortunato. This is the tour no one should miss and should be seen first. It provides a summary of the city's history and life.

Tour Routes 2, 3 and 4 allow the visitor to walk from the three major portals into Todi up the hill to the Piazza del Popolo. These three tours offer, in particular, a better understanding of medieval life in Todi and the urban structure that developed over centuries.

Tour Route 2 begins at Porta Perugina, the northern entry portal. **Tour Route 3** begins at Porta Romana, the southeastern entry point. **Tour 4** begins at the southwest base at Tempio della Consolazione, very near Porta Fratta, the oldest southern entry gate into Todi. These three routes all contains elements of all the major historical eras and coalesce at the top, the center of Todi, where it all began over 2,500 years ago.

TOUR ROUTE 1

(This tour takes between 2-3 hours. Parking is available at Porta Orvietana.)

TOUR ROUTE 1.
Piazza del Popolo

RIDE THE ELEVATOR to the top, then walk up via Ciuffelli to the piazza. You will walk by the Oberdan gardens on your immediate left. Pause here and partake of the beautiful view of the valley below toward the northwest.

View from Oberdan Gardens to western side of Todi known as nido dell aquila (eagle's nest), the site of the legendary founding of Todi (see POI-13)

Follow via Ciuffelli toward Piazza del Popolo, the social, political, religious, and commercial center of Todi. Along the road, you will see Renaissance palaces on both sides that typically date back to the sixteenth century.

For a brief side trip to one of the oldest districts of the city, the Valle Bassa, follow one of the very narrow streets downward to your left. Then return to via Ciuffelli and continue toward the piazza. The road widens and on your right, at the top of a large staircase, stands the imposing church of San Fortunato. At the base of the staircase, there is a small garden with a monument commemorating Jacopone da Todi (**POI-1**).

Continue toward the Piazza del Popolo. Bear left along the road, now called via Mazzini. On your right is the Teatro Comunale (**POI-2**).

Shortly, the road enters the Piazza del Popolo at the southwest corner (**POI-3**). We suggest you follow a clockwise course to see the rich sights on the piazza.

Walk toward the cathedral along the left side of the piazza. Almost immediately you will reach a narrow street on your left, via del Monte, that leads to the site of ancient Roman cisterns. You can walk down into this cavernous area to see where water was stored for over 2,000 years. Tickets are available at the southwest corner of the Piazza del Popolo, next to the *voltoni*, beneath the Palazzo del Capitano (see **POI-9, POI-10**).

Continue your walk to the cathedral (*il Duomo*) that stands on the north end of the piazza. It was built over the site of a Roman temple. Spend some time here to enjoy the many details of historic and artistic importance (**POI-4**).

As you descend the steps, walk around the side of the cathedral to your right. Notice the palace that nearly abuts the steps of the cathedral, and how its forward extension disrupts the symmetry of the piazza. Construction of this palace began in the mid-sixteenth century, immediately adjacent to the Cesi Palace, by the powerful Atti family. Its encroachment demonstrates the power of the family. The fact that the planned Atti palace would have greatly overshadowed the Cesi palace in size, and that it violated architectural rules, infuriated the Cesis. A terrible feud occurred between the two families that ended in tragedy in 1553. The Cesi family slaughtered nearly all of the Attis and construction ceased at the ground floor level. The palace was not completed until 1920.

As you follow along the side of the cathedral, you will pass Palazzo Cesi on your left, a typical example of a private Renaissance palace (**POI-5**).

Before the Bishop's Palace was built, it was the home of Bishop Angelo Cesi, one of the most important personalities in the history of Todi (**POI-6**).

Farther along you will reach the Bishop's Palace, a magnificent example of a Renaissance public place. It was commissioned by Bishop Cesi and can be visited by reservation (**POI-7**).

Walk back to the cathedral and proceed to the east side of the piazza. You will pass imposing palaces constructed as far back as the thirteenth century (**POI-8**).

Continuing your stroll, you will reach the political and administrative center of the city. Toward the end of the piazza on your left is the Palazzo del Capitano (**POI-9**), which is connected to the Palazzo del Popolo (**POI-10**).

Within the Palazzo del Popolo is an interesting museum (*pinoteca*) that houses amazing archaeological finds, documents and paintings of local interest. It includes a cast of the famous Mars statue (**POI-11**).

On the immediate southeast corner is the Palazzo del Priori (**POI-12, POI-13**).

In the southeast corner of the piazza is a smaller, but historically important piazza, the Piazza Garibaldi (**POI-14**).

At this point, it is worthwhile to relax at one of charming Caffè before proceeding to the church of San Fortunato. Look around you. Piazza del Popolo, the ancient town center for over two thousand years, has stood largely unchanged for well over one thousand years! It has been considered, arguably, as the most emblematic of hill town central piazzas in all Italy.

Now take a brief walk back out of the Piazza del Popolo down via Mazzini to the Church of San Fortunato (**POI-15**).

After exiting San Fortunato, before descending the staircase, take an immediate left turn. At the end of the church, turn left and walk up a narrow street. You will immediately reach the Liceo Jacopone da Todi (**POI-16**). It was built in the 13th–14th century as a Franciscan convent where fra Jacopone lived as a friar, then later in his life as a prisoner of Pope Boniface VIII. The current building was constructed on the site in 14th–15th centuries.

Now continue to walk up the road where you will reach Parco della Rocca which may have been the site of an artisan well discovered by Umbri almost 3,000 years ago (**POI-17**).

Walk through the park. As you reach the western

edge of the park, descend a few steps that are flanked by terracotta statues of recumbent lions. Follow the path to the right back to the Oberdan garden. A second option is to follow the path down into the woods, where the Beverly Pepper Sculpture Garden continues all the way to the bottom of the hill, across from the Tempio della Consolazione (see **POI-29**). If the Oberdan garden path is taken, you can proceed back up to the Piazza del Popolo, or you can take the elevator back to the parking lot.

Another option is to turn left at the Oberdan garden and walk down the main road (via Mazzini) to the Tempio (see **POI-29**). Note: if you choose not to take Route 4, now is the time to see this very important chiurch.

TOUR ROUTE 2

LEGEND

- WALKING ROUTE
- ELEVATOR
- ANCIENT WALLS
- PARKING

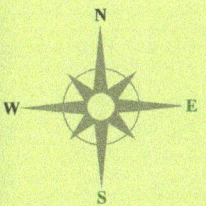

(This tour takes about 2 hours.
Parking is available across the road from the
entrance, at the Istituto Tecnico Agrario).

TOUR ROUTE 2.
From Porta Perugina to Piazza del Popolo

ENTER THE TOWN through the northern entrance, Porta Perugina. Before you enter through the portal on via Borgo Nuovo, pause for a moment to gain an appreciation of the medieval walls and gates and the structure of the medieval city (**POI-18**).

Now pass through the gate, where you will enter the Borgo Nuovo. This small neighborhood is still known as *Borgo Nuovo*, "the new village." During the Middle Ages, it was a very active place, inhabited by blacksmiths, weavers, carpenters, wood joiners and inlayers, and merchants (**POI-19**).

In recent times, this quaint neighborhood has shrunk considerably. However, like a lot of places, Borgo Nuovo has begun to reclaim its life, as immigrants from many parts of the world have begun to move into these historic homes.

Entering through the gate, a small church can be seen on the right, dedicated to Saint Eligio, the patron saint of blacksmiths. On the left, pass through the narrow via Fiorenzuola, and you will arrive at the large terrace of the bastione, now a playground for children and a place for adults to socialize. A wide panoramic view is evident from this terrace, looking east to the Martani Mountains, and north to the Tiber plain. Just outside the gate, to the north, one can see the tree-lined drive to Istituto Tecnico Agrario (**POI-20**)

Go back and rejoin via Borgo Nuovo. As you follow the steep street uphill, you will see examples of medieval houses. Numbers 87, 89, and 91 are typical (**POI-21**).

Proceed up the hill. After a short distance, past the imposing Saint Andrea Arch, you will reach number 30 on your left, the Monastery of Poor Clares with its famous painting Purgatorio inside the church (**POI-22**).

As you continue the walk, shortly you will pass through Porta di Santa Prassede, a gate that was part of the second set of walls, built by the Romans. A few yards ahead you will pass the Church of Santa Prassede (fourteenth century).

Take the left fork onto via Cesia o della Piana. You will arrive at Fonte Scannabecco, built in AD 1241 (**POI-23**).

As you continue, on your right you will pass Palazzo Pongelli (**POI-24**).

Next, you will pass the Church of Sant' Ilario (**POI-25**).

Now turn right onto via del Mercato Vecchio. On the left, you will pass the secondary entrance to Palazzo Francisci, a beautiful Renaissance palace that is now home to one of Europe's most advanced centers for the treatment of anorexia and other eating disorders. A short distance ahead in the Mercato Antico Piazza, you will see the Nicchioni Romani, dating from the first century BC (**POI-26**).

Now reverse your course along via Cesia o della Piana and turn left onto via del Teatro Antico. Halfway up the staircase, you can see a short stretch of Roman walls on your right. They are part of the remains of the Roman theater, which was originally accessed directly from the central forum, now known as Piazza del Popolo. Over the left-side wall, you can see a splendid panorama of the east side of Todi. You can imagine the view of theater goers in Roman times. The Roman theater was completely destroyed during the tumultuous centuries of barbarian invasion. Many of the huge stones were used to build the third set of walls along the base of the city, or were used in the construction of Christian churches and medieval or Renaissance palaces.

In the distance are the Martani Mountains. Along the foot of the mountain range, the original Roman road, via Flaminia, passed by from its source in Rome to Rimini, then toward central Europe.

Continue your walk through the impressive space, a set of open, arched rooms called voltoni, where you will enter the Piazza del Popolo (see **Tour Route 1**). As you enter the central square, you will have arrived at the most historic point in Todi—where it all began. Enjoy a *cappuccino con brioche, gelato*, or an *aperitif* at one of the *piazza caff*è and enjoy the scenery.

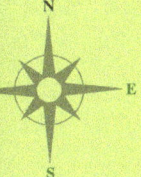

TOUR ROUTE 3

LEGEND

- WALKING ROUTE
- ELEVATOR
- ANCIENT WALLS
- PARKING

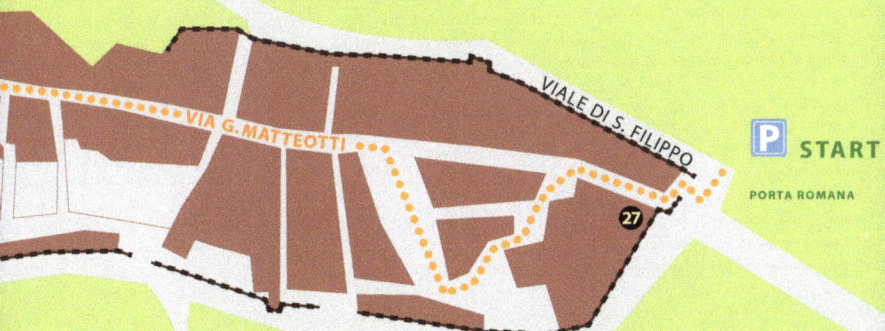

(This tour takes about 2 hours.
Parking is available just outside the gate).

TOUR ROUTE 3.

From Porta Romana to Piazza del Popolo

Enter through Porta Romana. At the gate, there are two sets of doors. The first, larger door was built in the sixteenth century in order to strengthen this important entrance to the city. Note the impressive stone construction *(bugnato)*. The second, smaller gate is the original medieval one, built in the thirteenth century. (**POI-27**).

On the left, continue down the narrow via dell'Anfiteatro, where you can see some remains of a Roman amphitheater (see POI-27). In the area around the ruins, objects and inscriptions related to Roman tombs have been found, as have remains of a Christian cemetery dating from the eleventh century. Continue along the via dell'Anfiteatro as it creates a U-turn back to via Matteotti.

Turn left and proceed up the hill along this main street and note the medieval homes on the left separated by herringbone alleys. Through these fascinating alleys, you can glimpse views of the valley and the hills beyond Todi.

Soon you will reach Porta Catena, which is part of the second set of walls, built by the Romans in the second century AD. Just before the portal, turn left and descend a few dozen steps onto the via di Mezzomuro, which follows along the original Roman wall (**POI-28**). Note the spectacular southeastern view over the lush valley that falls away from the town.

Go back up the steps to the main street, now called via Roma. Continue uphill for a short distance, then turn right onto via Cesia o della Piana. To your immediate left, you will see the fourteenth-century church of San Silvestro. Inside is the oldest, most faithful portrait of fra Jacopone (see **POI-1**), done by an unknown artist shortly after the poet's death.

Continue along the street. At number 65 on your left is a Renaissance palace called Palazzo Francisci, built in the sixteenth century. It now serves as home to an important center for the treatment of eating disorders. Shortly thereafter, on the same side of the street is the humble Sant'Ilario church (see **POI-25**), the Palazzo Pongelli (see **POI-24**), and the Scannabecco fountain (see **POI-23**).

Just before the Sant'Ilario church, turn left on via del Mercato Vecchio where you can admire the Roman Nicchioni (see **POI-26**).

Then turn right and continue on via Roma, where you will soon pass Porta Marzia, a gate that remains from its construction as part of the first circle of walls, built in the second century BC in the Etruscan-Roman era.

At this point the street is known as via Cavour. It is lined by Renaissance palaces, some of remarkable value. As you walk along, on your right is the Piazza di Marte, and on the left is the Piazza Bartolomeo d'Alviano.

Note the beautiful fountain in the rear of the piazza, commissioned by Bishop Angelo Cesi (see **POI-6**).

Soon you will reach the top of the hill, the center of town. On your right is Piazza Garibaldi (see **POI-14**) and straight ahead is the central square, Piazza del Popolo (see **POI-3**). At this point you will have reached the place where **Tour Route 1** takes you through the many historic sites around the central piazza. Stop at one of the many *caffè* and enjoy the sights!

(This tour takes about 2 hours. Parking is available at a short walking distance from the Tempio).

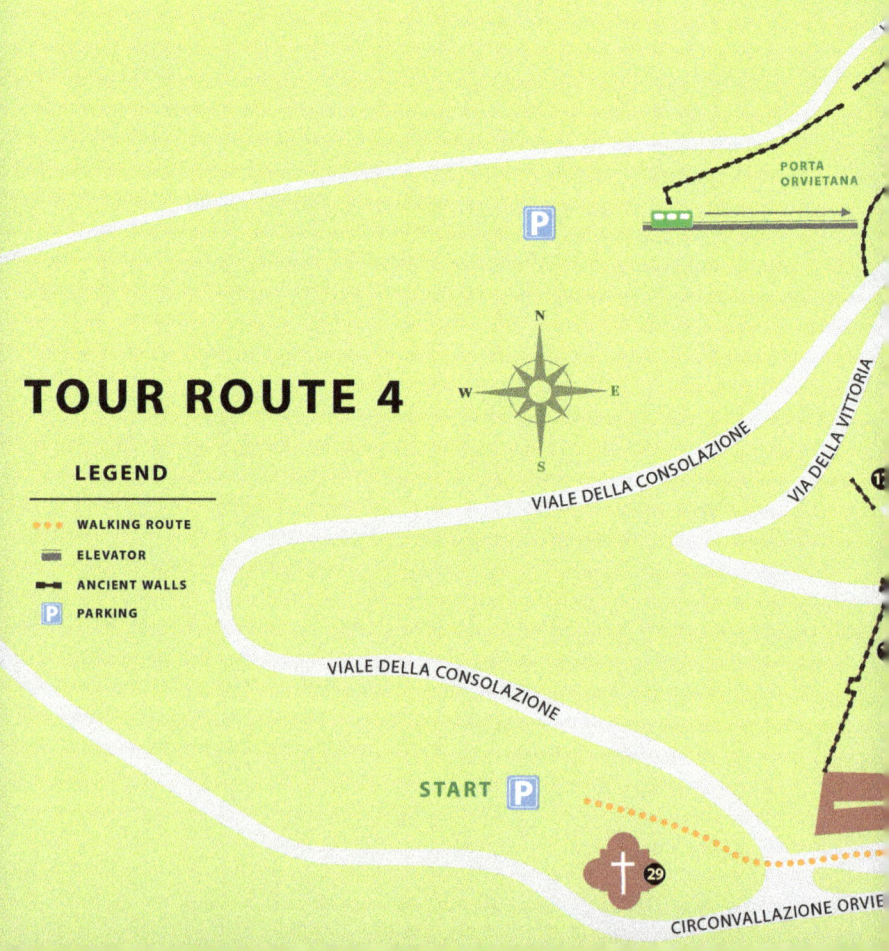

TOUR ROUTE 4.

From Tempio della Consolazione and Porta Fratta to Piazza del Popolo

As YOU STAND on the green space at the front of the temple and look east toward Todi, you can see remnants of the third circle of walls, both along the road to the east, as well as up the hill to your left (see **POI-18**). As you look left at the top of the hill, you will see the imposing bell tower of San Fortunato standing proudly.

Now enter the church and note its unique beauty. It is among the most significant representations of Renaissance architecture in all of Italy (**POI-29**).

As you exit, walk directly across the road to the east. Then walk along this wide road/parking area, known as via Abdon Menicali. Menicali was a nineteenth-century priest known for his creative interest in flying machines. He was also noted for his patriotic support of *Risorgimento*—the Italian unification movement—and was suspended from the Church for his "modernism." In 1886, Menicali attempted flight from the cliff high above on your left, la Rocca (see **POI-17**). Sadly, he failed and crashed to his death.

Continue walking as the street narrows somewhat and becomes via Beccaro. Shortly, you will reach a junction leading downhill to the right, a street known as via di Porta Fratta. Take a short stroll down the street. You will pass the church of San Giorgio, that dates to the year AD 1017, in a neighborhood of typical small medieval homes. At the bottom is Porta Fratta, once known as Porta Amerina. It is the oldest entrance to Todi, having been built by the Romans and recently restored. It led directly to Amelia, then continued south to other Roman towns on the way to Rome.

Turn around and walk back to via Beccaro, then turn right. You will immediately reach Porta Aurea, the "golden gate" of the second set of walls. Just before the gate, turn right and walk down a few steps to the via di Mezzomuro (see **POI-28**), which traverses the second set of walls. To the south, you will see a beautiful view of the valley sweeping below Todi. After twenty yards or so, turn back and retrace your steps to Porta Aurea, then follow the road as it continues uphill. After passing through the gate, the road name becomes via di S. Maria in Camuccia. Shortly, on your right you will come to a church of the same name, built in the seventh or eighth century AD (**POI-30**).

Continue walking until you reach the major road, via Roma. At this point, you can choose one of two directions. If you have already walked along **Tour Route 3**, turn left and walk up via Roma, which becomes via Cavour, until you reach the top, Piazza del Popolo.

Otherwise, turn right on via Roma for a very short distance, then turn left onto via Cesia o della Piana.

On your immediate left is the fourteenth-century church of San Silvestro. Inside is the oldest, most faithful portrait of fra Jacopone (see **POI-1**), done by an unknown artist shortly after the poet's death.

Continue along the street. At number 65 on your left is a Renaissance palace called Palazzo Francisci, built in the sixteenth century. It now serves as home to an important center for the treatment of eating disorders. Shortly thereafter on the same side of the street is the humble Sant'Ilario church (see **POI-25**), the Palazzo Pongelli (see **POI-24**) and the Scannabecco fountain (see **POI-23**). Just before the Sant'Ilario church, turn left on via del Mercato Vecchio, where you can admire the Roman Nicchioni (see **POI-26**).

Then turn right and continue along via Roma, where you will soon pass Porta Marzia, a gate that remains as part of the first circle of walls, built in the second century BC in the Roman-Etruscan era. Pause here to look at the stonework construction begun by the Etruscans and continued by the Romans. Contemplate how they succeeded in moving these massive stones from quarries twenty miles away, then up the steep hill to this site.

At this point, the street is known as via Cavour. It is lined by Renaissance palaces, some of remarkable value. As you walk along, on your right you will pass the Piazza di Marte, and on your left is the Piazza Bartolomeo d'Alviano. Note the beautiful fountain in the rear of the piazza, commissioned by Bishop Angelo Cesi (see **POI-6**).

Soon you will reach the top of the hill, the center of town. On your right is Piazza Garibaldi (see **POI-14**), and straight ahead is the central square, Piazza del Popolo (see **POI-3**).

PART IV
Interesting Historic Sites Near Todi

Introduction

Within a relatively short distance from Todi, one can find a number of beautiful representations of the history of Umbria, the "green heart of Italy." Specific examples are provided with a summary and driving directions.

Evidence of plant life (Petrified Forest) dates back over two million years. Colonization of the area by the Romans (Carsulae) offers a picture of human civilization dating back over two thousand years. As an example of life in this area during the Middle Ages, Montesanto provides the visitor with an opportunity to learn about the history of life in Todi and its environs.

The territory around Todi is dotted with a number of small villages, as well as medieval castles, nestled in the hills. These hamlets typically have one or more small restaurants and taverns that feature indigenous Umbrian food and wine. (See the reference Todi e i suoi Castelli for comprehensive details). These places are typically accessible by automobile along quaint, narrow roads that wind through the hills. Some examples include Massa Martana, Montecastello Vibio, Collazzone, Acquasparta, Montecastrilli and Baschi.

Some of these notable villages and castles are cited below with features that are unique to them.

Montesanto

(Directions: From the Tempio Consolazione, take the road east called Circonvallazione Orvietana, and follow signs to Convento di Montesanto. The distance from Todi is less than one mile.)

The church and convent of Montesanto stand atop a hill across the valley to the west of Todi. It is easily visible from the Oberdan garden on via A. Ciuffelli near the Piazza del Popolo. It was likely a sacred place dating back over 2,500 years or longer, during the time of the Etruscans, and was known in ancient times as Monte Mascarano, "monastery of the spirits." It was the location of various temples where rites were dedicated to deities. Close by, on a hill below Montesanto, the famous Mars statue was unearthed in 1835 (see **POI-11**).

The known history begins in AD 1235, when Santa Chiara (Saint Clare of Assisi) was still alive and the Monastery of the Poor Clares was built on the site. After about a century, the Poor Clares were moved and the building became a fortress of Cardinal Albornoz to defend Todi against attacks from the Orvieto direction. In 1450, it became a new monastery of the Franciscan friars and has remained so today, through turbulent times of expulsion and return.

The standing complex is medieval. Within the church are a number of interesting art works, particularly those done by the Italian high Renaissance painter Lo Spagna, so-called because of his Spanish birth. The original of his altar painting, The Coronation of the Virgin, can be found in the Municipal Museum of Todi. A beautiful wooden sculpture representing the Crucifixion can be seen in a chapel.

On the piazza in front of the convent is a linden tree planted in AD 1428 to honor a visit by Saint Bernardino of Sienna.

Carsulae

(Directions: From Todi, drive south on E45-S 3bis about 12 miles to San Gemini, where you will see signs to Carsulae).

Carsulae is a remarkable site dating back to 300 BC. It grew and thrived as a Roman town when a branch of the via Flaminia was constructed in 220 BC, one of the two major roads that led north from Rome.

The town was popular as a spa and was an active commercial site for a few hundred years, but then was abandoned for uncertain reasons in the fourth century AD, never to be rebuilt. The only remnant of post-Roman Carsulae is the small church of San Damiano, constructed in the eleventh century AD over the ruins of an old Roman building.

Carsulae was never actively destroyed despite falling into ruin. Today, remains of multiple Roman buildings can be seen, including an amphitheater, two twin temples, a public forum and baths, among others. Remarkably, the paved via Flaminia that passes through an intact arch at the northern end of the ancient town can still be seen as it traverses the center of Carsulae. Ruts from Roman carriages are still evident, created over a period of several hundred years.

Roman arch at northern entrance to Carsulae, dating back 2,000 years to the Augustan Era.

This amazing place is an unparalleled example of the remains of a Roman town that thrived in rural Umbria. Walking through the ruins of Carsulae easily brings to mind the legions of soldiers and citizens who traveled through the town heading north to Bevagna, a market town, passing by the eastern side of Todi almost 2,000 years ago.

Petrified Forest

(Directions: Take E 45- S 3bis south from Todi for several miles. Turn right at the exit toward Castigliano and follow the signs to Dunarobba. Total distance is less than 20 miles.)

Only a short distance south of Todi, near the village of Dunarobba, stands a fossil forest. First discovered in AD 1620, drawings of 200 fossilized stumps were made at this site. However, not until 1980 was a systematic effort made to study and preserve the remaining fifty trees, which date back over two million years.

Because these massive sequoia trees were buried in mud in the late Pliocene era, they are unique in that the trunks remained upright until their discovery in the last several hundred years. This location near Dunarobba was once a marshy area adjacent to a large lake that was gradually covered over by sandy clay sediment nearly two million years ago. The trees were encased in clay and became mummified, rather than petrified, over thousands of centuries. They offer one example of this phenomenon— with only three others in the entire world! In fact, the mummified wood actually still burns.

Today, visitors can walk through the site, which stands nearly unprotected in a fenced-off field. Considerable effort has been made to study and preserve these rare trees, but many stand beneath a crude, tent-like roof. It is not an overstatement to declare that these mummified trees are among the most important fossil findings in the world.

Notable Villages and Castles Near Todi:

(Directions: all the villages named below are within 2-5 miles, mostly south of Todi. Any map of Umbria will show the small roads that take you there.)

Camerata is in a beautiful setting with a medieval castle.

Cecanibbi is a small medieval village.

Colvalenza is an ancient village with a modern monastery founded by Mother Speranza, a holy Spanish nun who immigrated to the area in the twentieth century.

Duesanti is an ancient village with Roman remains and a beautiful church.

Fiore and Izzalini are close to Todi with beautiful castles

Montenero is a tiny village around a castle

Interesting Historic Sites Near Todi 119

Medieval Castle at the *frazione* Montenero
near Todi

Petroro has a recently restored castle and an ancient church

Torregentile has a castle and tower. Also, see the residence of the famous American sculptor, Beverly Pepper

Figure 5. Sketch of the numerous tiny villages (*frazioni*) that surround Todi

References

1. Carlo and Marco Grondona, *Todi storica e artistica*. Ediart, Todi, 2009
2. Franco Mancini. *Todi e i suoi castelli*. *Tipografia Tuderte*, second edition, 2012

Acknowledgments

We want to thank Bruno Ursini for his beautiful photographic contributions. We are especially grateful to Marcello Castrichini for sharing his extensive collection of photographs of Todi. We are grateful to our publisher, Gatekeeper Press, and its editors, artists, and other contributors. They made the complex process of publication look easy. We appreciate the input provided by the students of the Lyceum Jacopone da Todi for discussing, testing, and improving our recommended tour routes. Finally, we are thankful to many longstanding friends in Todi, especially Professor Marco Grondona, for offering gracious support of our endeavor.

www.ingramcontent.com/pod-product-compliance
Lightning Source LLC
LaVergne TN
LVHW072022060526
838200LV00058B/4649